GREEK YOGURT
Recipes

Publications International, Ltd.

Pictured on the front cover: Blueberry Yogurt Cake *(page 114)* and Mango Yogurt Drink *(page 23)*.

Pictured on the back cover *(left to right):* Greek Chicken Burgers with Cucumber Yogurt Sauce *(page 62)* and Maple Cinnamon Breakfast Parfaits *(page 10)*.

ISBN-13: 978-1-4508-6795-5
ISBN-10: 1-4508-6795-2

Library of Congress Control Number: 2013930799

Manufactured in China.

8 7 6 5 4 3 2 1

Nutritional Analysis: Every effort has been made to check the accuracy of the nutritional information that appears with each recipe. However, because numerous variables account for a wide range of values for certain foods, nutritive analyses in this book should be considered approximate. Different results may be obtained by using different nutrient databases and different brand-name products.

Microwave Cooking: Microwave ovens vary in wattage. Use the cooking times as guidelines and check for doneness before adding more time.

Note: This book is for informational purposes and is not intended to provide medical advice. Neither Publications International, Ltd., nor the authors, editors or publisher takes responsibility for any possible consequences from any treatment, procedure, exercise, dietary modification, action, or applications of medication or preparation by any person reading or following the information in this cookbook. The publication of this book does not constitute the practice of medicine, and this cookbook does not replace your physician, pharmacist or health-care specialist. **Before undertaking any course of treatment or nutritional plan, the authors, editors and publisher advise the reader to check with a physician or other health-care provider.**

Publications International, Ltd.

TABLE OF
CONTENTS

CULTURAL EDUCATION

What IS Greek Yogurt?

Everyone is talking about it. But what exactly is it? Like regular yogurt, Greek yogurt is made by adding active bacterial cultures to milk, causing it to ferment. What makes Greek yogurt different is that it's strained to remove most of the liquid whey, so it becomes thicker than American-style yogurt. Greek yogurt isn't only Greek—many cultures around the world have enjoyed strained yogurt for thousands of years.

Good and Good for You

Americans are just discovering what people in Europe and the Middle East have known for years—Greek yogurt is not only delicious, but it's incredibly healthy and surprisingly versatile. This thick, creamy yogurt has nearly double the amount of protein of regular yogurt—15 to 20 grams in a typical 6-ounce serving, compared to 9 grams in regular yogurt. It contains about half the carbs—5 to 7 grams per serving versus 13 to 17 grams in regular yogurt. Greek yogurt also has about half the sodium and less sugar. The flavor is pleasantly tangy and less acidic than regular yogurt, a result of much of the lactic acid being drained off with the whey. For the greatest health benefits, opt for the low-fat or nonfat versions—full-fat Greek yogurt contains a large amount of fat, much of which is saturated fat. Saturated fat is commonly found in butter, cheeses, meats and other animal products; it has been found to increase levels of LDL (bad) cholesterol that lodges in arteries and contributes to the risk of cardiovascular disease.

Beware of Imitators

Making traditional Greek yogurt is expensive, as it can require two to four times as much milk as regular yogurt. As the popularity of Greek yogurt has increased, some manufacturers have looked for ways to cut corners, and one way to save money is to skip the straining process. Instead, some companies add thickeners such as pectin, gelatin, cornstarch or milk protein concentrate to make their yogurts thicker. There is currently no legal definition of Greek yogurt, so products with this name may be thickened by any viable method (natural or not). Be sure to look at the ingredients and choose yogurts which don't contain these thickening agents. The ingredients should include milk and live, active cultures.

4

Yogurt for Breakfast, Lunch and Dinner

You may currently enjoy Greek yogurt in its simplest form—topped with nuts, granola, fruit and/or honey. And Greek yogurt does make a wonderful, healthy, protein-packed breakfast, lunch or snack, but it can be so much more. Following are a few new ways to think about Greek yogurt and all it can do:

• It can replace sour cream and mayonnaise in many recipes, so you can enjoy some of your favorite foods, such as potato salad, ranch dressing, vegetable dips or deviled eggs, with less fat and fewer calories. Try it on top of baked potatoes and Mexican dishes as well.

• You can add it to marinades, as the natural acidity of Greek yogurt helps tenderize meat and adds an extra layer of flavor.

• It can be added to sauces instead of sour cream or whipping cream. (While Greek yogurt doesn't curdle as easily as regular yogurt or sour cream, it shouldn't be added directly to boiling liquids. Stir a few tablespoons of the hot liquid into the Greek yogurt in a separate bowl, then stir this mixture back into the pan of hot sauce.)

• It can replace some of the milk, buttermilk, butter, oil or sour cream in baking recipes. It generally can't be substituted one-for-one for all of these ingredients, however; with such a high protein content, the addition of Greek yogurt can make some baked goods tough. Try the recipes in the Best Baking chapter (page 100) and experiment a little to discover the amounts that work in your recipes.

• It can act as an emulsifier in salad dressings, adding flavor and texture to oil and vinegar combinations.

• You can sweeten Greek yogurt slightly or mix it with melted chocolate to top cakes and cupcakes, replacing frosting which is much higher in fat, calories and carbs.

This book is filled with exciting new ideas for using Greek yogurt in appetizers, dips, soups, salads, smoothies, main dishes and desserts. Try a few recipes yourself and discover just how versatile—and delicious—Greek yogurt can be!

SMART STARTS

Banana Split Breakfast Bowl

2½ tablespoons sliced almonds

2½ tablespoons chopped walnuts

3 cups vanilla nonfat Greek yogurt

1⅓ cups sliced strawberries (about 12 medium)

2 bananas, cut in half and sliced lengthwise

½ cup drained pineapple tidbits

1. Spread almonds and walnuts in single layer in small heavy skillet. Cook and stir over medium heat 2 minutes or until lightly browned. Immediately remove from skillet; cool completely.

2. Spoon yogurt into four bowls. Top with strawberries, banana slices and pineapple. Sprinkle with toasted nuts. *Makes 4 servings*

Nutrients per Serving (1 breakfast bowl): Calories: 268, Total Fat: 5g, Saturated Fat: <1g, Protein: 10g, Carbohydrate: 50g, Cholesterol: 0mg, Fiber: 5g, Sodium: 112mg

Note: Breakfast is a great time to eat one of the two recommended fruit servings for the day. There's no need to put aside your favorite recipes until berry season comes around; recipes like this one can be made with fresh or frozen strawberries. Frozen fruits are economical, convenient and available year-round—they are harvested at their peak of ripeness and can be stored in the freezer for 8 to 12 months.

Whole Wheat Pancakes

¾ cup fat-free (skim) milk
2 eggs
¼ cup plain nonfat Greek yogurt
2 tablespoons vegetable oil
1 tablespoon honey
1 cup whole wheat flour
2 teaspoons baking powder
⅛ teaspoon salt
2 teaspoons butter
　Raspberries, blueberries and/or strawberries (optional)
　Maple syrup or agave nectar (optional)

1. Whisk milk, eggs, yogurt, oil and honey in medium bowl until well blended. Add flour, baking powder and salt; whisk just until blended.

2. Heat large nonstick skillet over medium heat. Add 1 teaspoon butter; brush to evenly coat skillet. Drop batter by ¼ cupfuls into skillet. Cook about 2 minutes or until tops of pancakes appear dull and bubbles form around edges. Turn and cook 1 to 2 minutes or until bottoms are firm and browned, adding remaining 1 teaspoon butter as needed.

3. Serve with berries and maple syrup, if desired.　　*Makes 4 servings*

Nutrients per Serving (3 pancakes): Calories: 260, Total Fat: 12g, Saturated Fat: 3g, Protein: 10g, Carbohydrate: 30g, Cholesterol: 100mg, Fiber: 3g, Sodium: 320mg

Tip: To keep pancakes warm while remaining batches are cooking, heat oven to 200°F and place a wire cooling rack directly on oven rack. Transfer pancakes to wire rack as they finish cooking. The pancakes will stay warm without getting soggy.

Maple Cinnamon Breakfast Parfaits

1½ cups vanilla nonfat Greek yogurt
1 banana, mashed
2 tablespoons maple syrup
¾ to 1 teaspoon ground cinnamon
1 cup honey-sweetened oat flakes cereal
½ cup flaked coconut
1 can (8 ounces) crushed pineapple in juice, drained
2 cups strawberries, quartered
1 kiwi, peeled and diced

1. Combine yogurt, banana, maple syrup and cinnamon in medium bowl; mix well.

2. Spoon about ⅓ cup yogurt mixture into each of four parfait glasses or bowls. Top with cereal, coconut and fruit.   *Makes 4 servings*

Nutrients per Serving (1 parfait): Calories: 340, Total Fat: 4g, Saturated Fat: 3g, Protein: 19g, Carbohydrate: 60g, Cholesterol: 0mg, Fiber: 6g, Sodium: 170mg

Variation: Substitute honey for maple syrup.

Tip: Prepare yogurt mixture the night before. Cover and refrigerate until ready to serve.

Fruit Kabobs with Raspberry Yogurt Dip
(pictured)

½ cup vanilla nonfat Greek yogurt
¼ cup no-sugar-added raspberry fruit spread
1 pint fresh strawberries
2 cups *each* cubed honeydew and cantaloupe (1-inch cubes)
1 can (8 ounces) pineapple chunks in juice, drained

1. Combine yogurt and fruit spread in small bowl; mix well.

2. Thread fruit alternately onto six 12-inch skewers. Serve with yogurt dip.

Makes 6 servings

Nutrients per Serving (1 kabob with 2 tablespoons dip): Calories: 120, Total Fat: 0g, Saturated Fat: 0g, Protein: 3g, Carbohydrate: 27g, Cholesterol: 0mg, Fiber: 2g, Sodium: 30mg

Honey-Nut Fruit Tumble

1 cup vanilla nonfat Greek yogurt
¼ cup rolled oats
¼ cup wheat germ
2 tablespoons orange juice
1 tablespoon honey
1 teaspoon grated orange peel
1 teaspoon lemon juice
2 cups chopped apples
½ cup *each* sliced strawberries, chopped peaches and blueberries
¼ cup chopped walnuts

1. Combine yogurt, oats, wheat germ, orange juice, honey, orange peel and lemon juice in medium bowl; mix well.

2. Gently stir in apples, strawberries, peaches, blueberries and walnuts. Refrigerate at least 2 hours or overnight.

Makes 8 servings

Nutrients per Serving (½ cup): Calories: 100, Total Fat: 3g, Saturated Fat: 0g, Protein: 5g, Carbohydrate: 16g, Cholesterol: 0mg, Fiber: 2g, Sodium: 15mg

English Muffin Breakfast Sandwiches

2 tablespoons plain nonfat Greek yogurt
1 tablespoon spicy brown or Dijon mustard
½ teaspoon dried tarragon or basil
4 English muffins, split
4 slices Canadian bacon
4 large tomato slices (about ¼ inch thick)
2 slices (1 ounce each) reduced-fat Swiss cheese, cut in half
4 Poached Eggs (recipe follows)
   Paprika (optional)

1. Preheat broiler.

2. Stir yogurt, mustard and tarragon in small bowl until well blended. Spread one fourth of yogurt mixture over each of four muffin halves. Top evenly with Canadian bacon, tomato and cheese. Place on broiler pan with remaining muffin halves.

3. Broil 4 inches from heat source 1 minute or until muffins are toasted and cheese just begins to brown. Place poached eggs on cheese-topped muffin halves and sprinkle with paprika, if desired. Top with remaining muffin halves. *Makes 4 servings*

Nutrients per Serving (1 breakfast sandwich): Calories: 300, Total Fat: 11g, Saturated Fat: 5g, Protein: 22g, Carbohydrate: 28g, Cholesterol: 210mg, Fiber: 2g, Sodium: 1070mg

Poached Eggs: Fill medium saucepan with about 1 quart water; bring to a boil over high heat. Add 2 tablespoons white vinegar and ½ teaspoon salt. Reduce heat to a simmer. Working with one egg at a time, crack egg into small bowl. Gently drop egg into simmering water. (Use a wooden spoon to budge egg gently to keep from sticking to bottom of saucepan.) Simmer 2 to 3 minutes or until white of egg is cooked through. Remove poached egg using slotted spoon. Repeat with remaining eggs.

Quick & Easy Tropical Parfait

1½ cups vanilla nonfat Greek yogurt
1 can (11 ounces) mandarin orange segments in light syrup, drained
　　and chopped
1 can (8 ounces) pineapple chunks in juice, drained
1 medium banana, sliced
2 tablespoons shredded coconut, toasted

1. Combine yogurt and oranges in medium bowl.

2. Spoon half of yogurt mixture into four serving bowls; top with pineapple. Spoon remaining yogurt mixture over pineapple; top with banana slices. Sprinkle with coconut. Serve immediately.

Makes 4 servings

Nutrients per Serving (1 parfait): Calories: 180, Total Fat: 1g, Saturated Fat: 1g, Protein: 9g, Carbohydrate: 36g, Cholesterol: 0mg, Fiber: 2g, Sodium: 45mg

Tip: Bananas are high in fiber, low in calories and a good source of vitamin B6, vitamin C and potassium. Choose fruit that is plump and evenly colored with no bruises or splits in the skin. Bananas with green tips and ridges will ripen at home within a day or two. They are ready to eat when the skin is deep yellow and studded with brown speckles.

Fabulous Feta Frittata

8 eggs
¼ cup plain nonfat Greek yogurt
¼ cup chopped fresh basil
¼ teaspoon salt
¼ teaspoon black pepper
1 tablespoon olive oil or butter
1 package (4 ounces) crumbled feta cheese with basil, olives and
    sun-dried tomatoes *or* 1 cup crumbled plain feta cheese
¼ cup pine nuts (optional)

1. Preheat broiler. Whisk eggs, yogurt, basil, salt and pepper in medium bowl until well blended.

2. Heat oil in large ovenproof skillet over medium heat, tilting skillet to coat bottom and side. Pour egg mixture into skillet; cover and cook 8 to 10 minutes or until eggs are set around edge (center will be wet).

3. Sprinkle feta and pine nuts, if desired, evenly over top. Transfer to broiler; broil 4 to 5 inches from heat source 2 minutes or until center is set and pine nuts are golden brown. Cut into wedges.

Makes 4 servings

Nutrients per Serving (¼ of total recipe): Calories: 270, Total Fat: 20g, Saturated Fat: 8g, Protein: 21g, Carbohydrate: 3g, Cholesterol: 395mg, Fiber: 1g, Sodium: 670mg

Cornmeal Pancakes

1½ cups yellow cornmeal
¾ cup all-purpose flour
1½ teaspoons baking powder
1 teaspoon salt
1⅓ cups plain nonfat Greek yogurt
⅔ cup fat-free (skim) milk
2 eggs, lightly beaten
¼ cup sugar
2 tablespoons plus 2 teaspoons butter, melted, divided
    Blueberries (optional)
    Maple syrup (optional)

1. Combine cornmeal, flour, baking powder and salt in medium bowl. Whisk yogurt, milk, eggs, sugar and 2 tablespoons butter in large bowl until well blended. Stir cornmeal mixture into yogurt mixture; let stand 5 minutes.

2. Brush griddle or large skillet with 1 teaspoon butter; heat over medium heat. Drop batter by ⅓ cupfuls onto griddle. Cook 3 minutes or until tops of pancakes are bubbly and appear dry. Turn and cook 2 minutes or until bottoms are golden, adding remaining 1 teaspoon butter as needed. Serve with blueberries and maple syrup, if desired. *Makes 4 servings*

Nutrients per Serving (¼ of total recipe): Calories: 480, Total Fat: 11g, Saturated Fat: 6g, Protein: 18g, Carbohydrate: 75g, Cholesterol: 115mg, Fiber: 4g, Sodium: 1610mg

SENSATIONAL
SMOOTHIES

Mango Yogurt Drink
(pictured)

1 ripe mango, sliced
½ cup vanilla nonfat Greek yogurt
¼ to ⅓ cup orange juice
1 teaspoon honey
2 ice cubes

1. Combine mango, yogurt, ¼ cup orange juice, honey and ice in blender; blend until smooth. Add additional orange juice, if necessary, to reach desired consistency.

2. Pour into two glasses. Serve immediately.   *Makes 2 servings*

Nutrients per Serving (¾ cup): Calories: 170, Total Fat: 1g, Saturated Fat: 0g, Protein: 7g, Carbohydrate: 36g, Cholesterol: 0mg, Fiber: 3g, Sodium: 30mg

Black Forest Smoothie

1 container (6 ounces) vanilla nonfat Greek yogurt
½ cup frozen dark sweet cherries
¼ cup fat-free (skim) milk
2 tablespoons sugar
2 tablespoons unsweetened cocoa powder
¼ teaspoon almond extract
1 to 2 ice cubes

1. Combine yogurt, cherries, milk, sugar, cocoa, almond extract and ice in blender; blend until smooth.

2. Pour into two glasses. Serve immediately.   *Makes 2 servings*

Nutrients per Serving (¾ cup): Calories: 100, Total Fat: 0g, Saturated Fat: 0g, Protein: 10g, Carbohydrate: 15g, Cholesterol: 0mg, Fiber: 1g, Sodium: 50mg

Spiced Maple Banana Oatmeal Smoothie
(pictured)

½ cup ice cubes
1 frozen banana
¼ cup fat-free (skim) milk
½ cup vanilla nonfat Greek yogurt
¼ cup quick oats
1 tablespoon maple syrup, plus additional for garnish
⅛ teaspoon ground cinnamon
⅛ teaspoon ground nutmeg
Whipped cream and cinnamon stick (optional)

1. Crush ice in blender.

2. Add banana and milk; blend until smooth. Add yogurt, oats, 1 tablespoon maple syrup, cinnamon and nutmeg; blend until smooth.

3. Pour into two glasses. Garnish with whipped cream, cinnamon stick and additional maple syrup. *Makes 2 servings*

Nutrients per Serving: Calories: 170, Total Fat: 1g, Saturated Fat: 0g, Protein: 9g, Carbohydrate: 33g, Cholesterol: 0mg, Fiber: 3g, Sodium: 40mg

Kiwi Strawberry Smoothie

2 kiwi, peeled and sliced
1 cup frozen unsweetened strawberries
1 container (6 ounces) vanilla nonfat Greek yogurt
½ cup low-fat (1%) milk
2 tablespoons honey

1. Combine kiwi, strawberries, yogurt, milk and honey in blender; blend until smooth.

2. Pour into two glasses. Serve immediately. *Makes 2 servings*

Nutrients per Serving (1 cup): Calories: 210, Total Fat: 0g, Saturated Fat: 0g, Protein: 11g, Carbohydrate: 44g, Cholesterol: 0mg, Fiber: 4g, Sodium: 70mg

Honeydew Ginger Smoothie
(pictured)

1½ cups cubed honeydew melon
½ cup sliced banana
½ cup vanilla nonfat Greek yogurt
½ cup ice cubes (about 4)
¼ teaspoon grated ginger

1. Combine honeydew, banana, yogurt, ice and ginger in blender; blend until smooth.

2. Pour into three glasses. Serve immediately.   *Makes 3 servings*

Nutrients per Serving (1 cup): Calories: 80, Total Fat: 0g, Saturated Fat: 0g, Protein: 4g, Carbohydrate: 16g, Cholesterol: 0mg, Fiber: 1g, Sodium: 30mg

Berry Morning Medley

1½ cups fat-free (skim) milk
1 cup frozen mixed berries
½ cup vanilla nonfat Greek yogurt
1 tablespoon sugar
¼ teaspoon vanilla
¼ cup granola

1. Combine milk and berries in blender; blend until mixture is thick and creamy. Add yogurt, sugar and vanilla; blend until smooth. Add granola; pulse 15 to 20 seconds.

2. Pour into two glasses. Serve immediately.   *Makes 2 servings*

Nutrients per Serving: Calories: 190, Total Fat: 2g, Saturated Fat: 0g, Protein: 13g, Carbohydrate: 33g, Cholesterol: 5mg, Fiber: 3g, Sodium: 105mg

Cinnamon-Apple Smoothie
(pictured)

2 Gala, Braeburn or other apples, peeled and sliced
2 cups ice cubes or crushed ice
2 bananas, sliced
1 container (6 ounces) vanilla nonfat Greek yogurt
¾ cup apple juice
2 teaspoons ground cinnamon, plus additional for garnish
   Whipped cream (optional)

1. Reserve 4 apple slices for garnish. Combine remaining apples, ice, bananas, yogurt, apple juice and 2 teaspoons cinnamon in blender; blend until smooth.

2. Pour into four glasses. Garnish with whipped cream, reserved apple slices and additional cinnamon. *Makes 4 servings*

Nutrients per Serving: Calories: 130, Total Fat: 0g, Saturated Fat: 0g, Protein: 5g, Carbohydrate: 30g, Cholesterol: 0mg, Fiber: 3g, Sodium: 25mg

Cherry Vanilla Chilla

2 ice cubes
¾ cup vanilla nonfat Greek yogurt
¾ cup frozen cherries
½ cup fat-free (skim) milk
2 teaspoons sugar
1½ teaspoons vanilla

1. Crush ice in blender.

2. Add yogurt, cherries, milk, sugar and vanilla; blend until smooth. Pour into two glasses. Serve immediately. *Makes 2 servings*

Nutrients per Serving: Calories: 140, Total Fat: 0g, Saturated Fat: 0g, Protein: 10g, Carbohydrate: 22g, Cholesterol: 0mg, Fiber: 1g, Sodium: 65mg

Raspberry Smoothie
(pictured)

1½ cups fresh or frozen raspberries
1 cup vanilla nonfat Greek yogurt
1 tablespoon honey
1 cup crushed ice

1. Combine raspberries, yogurt, honey and ice in blender; blend until smooth.

2. Pour into two glasses. Serve immediately.   *Makes 2 servings*

Nutrients per Serving (1½ cups): Calories: 160, Total Fat: 1g, Saturated Fat: 0g, Protein: 12g, Carbohydrate: 28g, Cholesterol: 0mg, Fiber: 6g, Sodium: 50mg

Island Delight Smoothie

2 cups chopped fresh or jarred mango
1 container (16 ounces) vanilla nonfat Greek yogurt
1½ cups pineapple-orange juice, chilled
1½ cups ice cubes
1 cup chopped pineapple
1 frozen banana
½ cup sliced fresh strawberries
2 tablespoons honey

1. Combine mango, yogurt, pineapple-orange juice, ice, pineapple, banana, strawberries and honey in blender; blend until smooth.

2. Pour into four glasses. Serve immediately.   *Makes 4 servings*

Nutrients per Serving: Calories: 260, Total Fat: 1g, Saturated Fat: 0g, Protein: 12g, Carbohydrate: 55g, Cholesterol: 0mg, Fiber: 3g, Sodium: 60mg

Peachy Vanilla Smoothie
(pictured)

1 medium peach, peeled and pitted
¾ cup fat-free (skim) milk
½ cup crushed ice
¼ cup plain nonfat Greek yogurt
1 tablespoon sugar
½ teaspoon vanilla

1. Combine peach, milk, ice, yogurt, sugar and vanilla in blender; blend until smooth.

2. Pour into two glasses. Serve immediately.   *Makes 2 servings*

Nutrients per Serving (¾ cup): Calories: 110, Total Fat: 0g, Saturated Fat: 0g, Protein: 6g, Carbohydrate: 20g, Cholesterol: 0mg, Fiber: 1g, Sodium: 120mg

Light Lemon Strawberry Smoothie

1 cup frozen unsweetened strawberries
¾ cup fat-free (skim) milk
1 tablespoon lemon juice
½ cup vanilla nonfat Greek yogurt
2 ice cubes (optional)

1. Combine strawberries, milk and lemon juice in blender; blend until smooth. Add yogurt; blend until smooth. For thicker consistency, add ice; blend until smooth.

2. Pour into two glasses. Serve immediately.   *Makes 2 servings*

Nutrients per Serving: Calories: 100, Total Fat: 0g, Saturated Fat: 0g, Protein: 9g, Carbohydrate: 16g, Cholesterol: 0mg, Fiber: 2g, Sodium: 65mg

Blueberry Banana Oatmeal Smoothie
(pictured)

1 cup reduced-fat (2%) milk
½ cup frozen blueberries
1 banana, sliced
½ cup plain nonfat Greek yogurt
¼ cup quick oats

1. Combine milk, blueberries and banana in blender; blend until smooth. Add yogurt and oats; blend until smooth.

2. Pour into two glasses. Serve immediately. *Makes 2 servings*

Nutrients per Serving: Calories: 200, Total Fat: 2g, Saturated Fat: 0g, Protein: 6g, Carbohydrate: 20g, Cholesterol: 0mg, Fiber: 1g, Sodium: 120mg

Spiced Passion Fruit Smoothie

1 cup vanilla nonfat Greek yogurt
1 cup sliced fresh strawberries
1 banana, sliced
¼ cup frozen passion fruit juice concentrate, thawed
¾ teaspoon pumpkin pie spice
⅛ teaspoon white pepper

1. Combine yogurt, strawberries, banana, juice concentrate, pumpkin pie spice and white pepper in blender; blend until smooth

2. Pour into three glasses. Serve immediately. *Makes 3 servings*

Nutrients per Serving (¾ cup): Calories: 110, Total Fat: <1g, Saturated Fat: 0g, Protein: 6g, Carbohydrate: 23g, Cholesterol: 0mg, Fiber: 2g, Sodium: 65mg

Energy Smoothie
(pictured)

1 package (16 ounces) frozen unsweetened strawberries,
    partially thawed
2 bananas, sliced
1 container (6 ounces) vanilla nonfat Greek yogurt
1 cup vanilla soymilk or milk*
⅓ cup powdered sugar
2 teaspoons vanilla

If using milk, add 1 to 2 tablespoons additional sugar, if desired.

1. Combine strawberries, bananas, yogurt, soymilk, powdered sugar and vanilla in blender; blend until smooth.

2. Pour into four glasses. Serve immediately.   *Makes 4 servings*

Nutrients per Serving (1 cup): Calories: 190, Total Fat: 1g, Saturated Fat: 0g, Protein: 7g, Carbohydrate: 40g, Cholesterol: 0mg, Fiber: 4g, Sodium: 45mg

Peanut Butter Banana Blend

1 frozen banana
½ cup vanilla nonfat Greek yogurt
½ cup fat-free (skim) milk
1 tablespoon natural unsweetened peanut butter

1. Combine banana, yogurt, milk and peanut butter in blender; blend until smooth.

2. Pour into two glasses. Serve immediately.   *Makes 2 servings*

Nutrients per Serving: Calories: 160, Total Fat: 4g, Saturated Fat: 1g, Protein: 10g, Carbohydrate: 22g, Cholesterol: 0mg, Fiber: 2g, Sodium: 90mg

APPETIZERS & SNACKS

Micro Mini Stuffed Potatoes

1 pound small new red potatoes
¼ cup plain nonfat Greek yogurt
1 tablespoon butter, softened
½ teaspoon minced garlic
¼ cup fat-free (skim) milk
½ cup (2 ounces) shredded reduced-fat sharp Cheddar cheese
½ teaspoon salt
¼ teaspoon black pepper
¼ cup finely chopped green onions (optional)

1. Pierce potatoes with fork in several places. Microwave potatoes on HIGH 5 to 6 minutes or until tender. Let stand 5 minutes; cut in half lengthwise. Scoop out pulp from potatoes; set potato shells aside.

2. Beat potato pulp in medium bowl with electric mixer at low speed 30 seconds. Add yogurt, butter and garlic; beat until well blended. Gradually add milk, beating until smooth. Add cheese, salt and pepper; beat until blended.

3. Fill potato shells with potato mixture. Microwave on HIGH 1 to 2 minutes or until cheese melts. Garnish with green onions.

Makes 4 servings

Nutrients per Serving (¼ of total recipe): Calories: 160, Total Fat: 6g, Saturated Fat: 4g, Protein: 7g, Carbohydrate: 20g, Cholesterol: 20mg, Fiber: 2g, Sodium: 440mg

Creamy Dill Cheese Spread
(pictured)

2 tablespoons garlic and herb spreadable cheese
1 tablespoon light mayonnaise
1 tablespoon plain nonfat Greek yogurt
1 to 2 teaspoons chopped fresh dill
⅛ teaspoon salt (optional)
24 garlic-flavored melba rounds

1. Combine cream cheese, mayonnaise, yogurt, dill and salt, if desired, in small bowl; mix well. Cover and refrigerate 1 hour.

2. Top each melba round with ½ teaspoon spread.

Makes 4 servings

Nutrients per Serving (6 topped melba rounds): Calories: 150, Total Fat: 8g, Saturated Fat: 4g, Protein: 7g, Carbohydrate: 17g, Cholesterol: 15mg, Fiber: 2g, Sodium: 380mg

Berry Good Dip

8 ounces fresh strawberries or frozen unsweetened strawberries, thawed
4 ounces light cream cheese, softened
¼ cup plain nonfat Greek yogurt
1 tablespoon sugar
   Fresh fruit, such as apple slices, strawberries, pineapple wedges
      and orange segments

1. Place strawberries in food processor or blender; process until smooth.

2. Beat cream cheese in medium bowl until smooth. Stir in yogurt, strawberry purée and sugar until well blended. Cover and refrigerate until ready to serve.

3. Spoon dip into small serving bowl; serve with assorted fruit.

Makes 6 servings

Nutrients per Serving (¼ cup dip): Calories: 60, Total Fat: 3g, Saturated Fat: 2g, Protein: 3g, Carbohydrate: 7g, Cholesterol: 10mg, Fiber: 1g, Sodium: 95mg

Turkey Meatballs with Yogurt-Cucumber Sauce

2 tablespoons olive oil, divided
1 cup finely chopped onion
2 cloves garlic, minced
1¼ pounds lean ground turkey or ground lamb
½ cup plain dry bread crumbs
¼ cup whipping cream
1 egg, lightly beaten
3 tablespoons chopped fresh mint
1 teaspoon salt
⅛ teaspoon ground red pepper
    Yogurt-Cucumber Sauce (recipe follows)

1. Line two baking sheets with parchment paper. Heat 1 tablespoon oil in medium skillet over medium-high heat. Add onion; cook and stir 3 minutes or until softened. Add garlic; cook and stir 30 seconds. Cool slightly.

2. Combine turkey, onion mixture, bread crumbs, cream, egg, mint, salt and red pepper in large bowl; mix well. Shape mixture into 40 meatballs; place on prepared baking sheets. Cover with plastic wrap and refrigerate 1 hour.

3. Meanwhile, prepare Yogurt-Cucumber Sauce. Preheat oven to 400°F. Brush meatballs with remaining tablespoon oil. Bake 15 to 20 minutes, turning once during baking. Serve with sauce.   *Makes 8 servings*

Nutrients per Serving (5 meatballs and 2 tablespoons sauce): Calories: 210, Total Fat: 12g, Saturated Fat: 4g, Protein: 18g, Carbohydrate: 9g, Cholesterol: 75mg, Fiber: 1g, Sodium: 480mg

Yogurt-Cucumber Sauce: Combine 1 container (6 ounces) plain nonfat Greek yogurt, ½ cup peeled, seeded and finely chopped cucumber, 2 teaspoons grated lemon peel, 2 teaspoons lemon juice, 2 teaspoons chopped fresh mint and ¼ teaspoon salt in medium bowl; mix well. Refrigerate until ready to serve.

Hot and Spicy Hummus

1 can (about 15 ounces) pinto beans, rinsed and drained
¼ cup plain nonfat Greek yogurt
2 teaspoons lemon juice
1 clove garlic, smashed
1 teaspoon chopped chipotle peppers in adobo sauce*
1 teaspoon olive oil
½ teaspoon ground cumin
¼ teaspoon salt
¼ teaspoon black pepper
2 to 3 tablespoons water (optional)
   Celery and carrot sticks (optional)

*Store the leftover chipotle peppers in adobo sauce in small containers in the freezer.

1. Combine beans, yogurt, lemon juice, garlic, chipotle pepper, oil, cumin, salt and black pepper in food processor or blender; process until smooth.

2. Add 2 to 3 tablespoons water, if needed, to reach desired consistency. Serve with vegetables, if desired.   *Makes 10 servings*

Nutrients per Serving (2 tablespoons): Calories: 40, Total Fat: 1g, Saturated Fat: 0g, Protein: 3g, Carbohydrate: 6g, Cholesterol: 0mg, Fiber: 2g, Sodium: 210mg

Tip: Try using this dip as a sandwich spread or in place of mayonnaise in tuna salad.

Dilly Deviled Eggs

6 hard-cooked eggs, peeled and cut in half lengthwise
2 tablespoons plain low-fat Greek yogurt
1 tablespoon light mayonnaise
1 tablespoon minced fresh dill *or* 1 teaspoon dried dill weed
1 tablespoon minced dill pickle
1 teaspoon Dijon mustard
⅛ teaspoon salt
⅛ teaspoon white pepper
  Paprika (optional)
  Dill sprigs (optional)

1. Remove yolks from egg halves. Mash yolks with yogurt, mayonnaise, dill, pickle, mustard, salt and pepper in small bowl.

2. Fill egg halves with mixture using teaspoon or piping bag fitted with large plain tip. Garnish with paprika and dill sprigs.   *Makes 6 servings*

Nutrients per Serving (2 egg halves): Calories: 80, Total Fat: 6g, Saturated Fat: 2g, Protein: 7g, Carbohydrate: 1g, Cholesterol: 185mg, Fiber: 0g, Sodium: 170mg

Tip: For hard-cooked eggs, place the eggs in a single layer in a saucepan. Add cold water to cover the eggs by 1 inch; cover and bring to a boil over high heat. Remove from the heat and let stand 15 minutes. Immediately pour off the water, cover with cold water and let stand until cooled. To peel, crack the shell all over by tapping the egg on the counter. Gently roll the egg across the counter with the palm of your hand to loosen the shell, then peel it away under cold running water.

Persian Eggplant Dip

3 large eggplants (3½ pounds total), peeled and cut into 1-inch cubes
1 teaspoon salt
5 tablespoons extra virgin olive oil, divided
2 onions, chopped
1 tablespoon dried mint
3 tablespoons plain nonfat Greek yogurt
⅓ cup finely chopped walnuts
    Pita bread wedges, carrots and sugar snap peas

1. Toss eggplant with salt in large bowl; transfer to large colander. Place colander in large bowl or sink and let stand 1 hour at room temperature to drain.

2. Heat 1 tablespoon oil in large nonstick skillet over medium-high heat. Add onions; cook and stir 5 to 6 minutes or until lightly browned. Transfer to slow cooker. Stir in eggplant. Cover; cook on LOW 6 to 8 hours or on HIGH 3½ to 4 hours or until eggplant is very soft.

3. Heat remaining 4 tablespoons oil in small saucepan over low heat. Add mint; cook about 15 minutes or until very fragrant. Set aside to cool slightly.

4. Transfer eggplant and onions to colander or fine mesh strainer with slotted spoon and press out any excess liquid with back of spoon. Return to slow cooker; mash with fork. Stir in yogurt. Sprinkle with chopped walnuts; drizzle with mint oil. Serve warm with pita bread and vegetables.

Makes 12 to 16 servings

Nutrients per Serving: Calories: 110, Total Fat: 8g, Saturated Fat: 1g, Protein: 2g, Carbohydrate: 9g, Cholesterol: 0mg, Fiber: 5g, Sodium: 200mg

Tuna Cakes with Creamy Cucumber Sauce

½ cup finely chopped cucumber
½ cup plain nonfat Greek yogurt
1½ teaspoons chopped fresh dill *or* ½ teaspoon dried dill weed
1 teaspoon lemon-pepper seasoning
⅓ cup shredded carrots
¼ cup sliced green onions
¼ cup finely chopped celery
¼ cup reduced-fat mayonnaise
2 teaspoons spicy brown mustard
1 cup panko bread crumbs, divided
1 can (12 ounces) albacore tuna in water, drained
1 tablespoon canola oil or olive oil, divided
Lemon wedges (optional)

1. For sauce, combine cucumber, yogurt, dill and lemon-pepper seasoning in small bowl; mix well. Cover and refrigerate until ready to serve.

2. Combine carrots, green onions, celery, mayonnaise and mustard in medium bowl. Stir in ½ cup panko. Stir in tuna until blended.

3. Place remaining ½ cup panko in shallow dish. Shape tuna mixture into 5 (½-inch-thick) patties. Dip patties in panko, coating lightly.

4. Heat 1½ teaspoons oil in large skillet over medium heat. Add patties; cook 5 to 6 minutes or until golden brown, turning once and adding remaining 1½ teaspoons oil to skillet when turning patties. Serve with sauce and lemon wedges, if desired. *Makes 5 servings*

Nutrients per Serving (1 tuna cake and 2 tablespoons sauce): Calories: 220, Total Fat: 8g, Saturated Fat: 1g, Protein: 20g, Carbohydrate: 15g, Cholesterol: 35mg, Fiber: 1g, Sodium: 350mg

Harvest Sticks with Vegetable Dip

1 container (8 ounces) reduced-fat cream cheese with chives spread, softened
1 cup plain nonfat Greek yogurt
⅓ cup finely chopped cucumber
2 tablespoons chopped fresh parsley
2 tablespoons dry minced onion *or* ¼ cup finely chopped fresh onion
1 clove garlic, minced
½ teaspoon curry powder (optional)
¼ teaspoon salt
6 large carrots, peeled
3 medium zucchini
  Raffia (optional)

1. Beat cream cheese in small bowl until fluffy; blend in yogurt. Stir in cucumber, parsley, onion, garlic, curry powder, if desired, and salt. Spoon into small serving bowl. Cover and refrigerate 1 hour or until ready to serve.

2. Cut carrots lengthwise into thin strips; gather into bundles. Tie raffia around bundles to hold in place, if desired. Repeat with zucchini. Serve with dip.   *Makes about 2 cups dip*

Nutrients per Serving (2 tablespoons dip): Calories: 50, Total Fat: 2g, Saturated Fat: 2g, Protein: 3g, Carbohydrate: 5g, Cholesterol: 5mg, Fiber: 1g, Sodium: 135mg

Note: The vegetable bundles can be made ahead of time. Cut vegetables as directed. Place carrots in medium bowl; cover with cold water and refrigerate until ready to use. Place zucchini sticks in small resealable plastic food storage bag and refrigerate until ready to use. Just before serving, gather vegetables into bundles and tie with raffia.

Cheesy Potato Skin Appetizers

5 baking potatoes (4 to 5 ounces each)
   Butter-flavored cooking spray
4 ounces light cream cheese, softened
2 tablespoons plain nonfat Greek yogurt
⅔ cup prepared salsa
⅓ cup shredded reduced-fat sharp Cheddar cheese
2 tablespoons sliced black olives (optional)
¼ cup minced fresh cilantro

1. Preheat oven to 425°F. Scrub potatoes; pierce several times with fork. Bake 45 minutes or until tender when pierced with fork. Let stand until cool enough to handle.

2. Cut each potato in half lengthwise. Scoop out pulp with spoon, leaving ¼-inch-thick shell. (Reserve pulp for another use, if desired.) Place potato skins on baking sheet; spray lightly with cooking spray.

3. Preheat broiler. Broil potato skins 6 inches from heat 5 minutes or until lightly browned and crisp.

4. *Reduce oven temperature to 350°F.* Combine cream cheese and yogurt in small bowl; mix well. Divide evenly among potato skins; top with salsa, Cheddar cheese and olives, if desired. Bake 15 minutes or until heated through. Sprinkle with cilantro. *Makes 10 servings*

Nutrients per Serving (1 potato skin appetizer): Calories: 120, Total Fat: 3g, Saturated Fat: 2g, Protein: 4g, Carbohydrate: 20g, Cholesterol: 10mg, Fiber: 2g, Sodium: 200mg

SAVORY
FAVORITES

Grilled Chipotle Chicken Sandwiches

½ cup plain nonfat Greek yogurt

2 tablespoons light mayonnaise

1 canned chipotle pepper in adobo sauce

2 teaspoons adobo sauce from canned chipotle

⅛ teaspoon salt (optional)

1 medium lime, halved

4 boneless skinless chicken breasts (4 ounces each), flattened slightly
   Black pepper

2 slices reduced-fat Swiss cheese, cut in half diagonally

4 whole wheat hamburger buns, split

4 leaves romaine lettuce

4 thin slices red onion

1. Spray grid with nonstick cooking spray; prepare grill for direct cooking.

2. Combine yogurt, mayonnaise, chipotle pepper, adobo sauce and salt, if desired, in food processor or blender; process until smooth.

3. Squeeze juice from one lime half evenly over chicken. Grill over medium-high heat 10 minutes. Turn chicken; sprinkle with black pepper. Grill 10 minutes or until chicken is cooked through (165°F).

4. Move chicken to side of grill. Squeeze remaining lime half over chicken; top with cheese. Place buns on grill, cut sides down; grill until lightly toasted.

5. Arrange lettuce, chicken and onion on bottom halves of buns. Spread top halves of buns with chipotle mixture; close sandwiches.

Makes 4 servings

Nutrients per Serving (1 sandwich): Calories: 350, Total Fat: 11g, Saturated Fat: 3g, Protein: 35g, Carbohydrate: 29g, Cholesterol: 85mg, Fiber: 5g, Sodium: 1670mg

Fettuccine Gorgonzola with Sun-Dried Tomatoes

4 ounces sun-dried tomatoes (not packed in oil)
8 ounces uncooked spinach or tri-color fettuccine
1 cup low-fat (1%) cottage cheese
½ cup plain nonfat Greek yogurt
½ cup (2 ounces) crumbled Gorgonzola cheese, plus additional
    for garnish
⅛ teaspoon white pepper

1. Place sun-dried tomatoes in small bowl; add hot water to cover. Let stand 15 minutes or until tomatoes are soft. Drain well; cut into strips.

2. Cook pasta according to package directions; drain. Cover and keep warm.

3. Meanwhile, combine cottage cheese and yogurt in food processor or blender; process until smooth. Heat cottage cheese mixture in large skillet over low heat. Add Gorgonzola cheese and pepper; stir until cheese is melted.

4. Add pasta and tomatoes to skillet; toss to coat with sauce. Garnish with additional Gorgonzola cheese; serve immediately.   *Makes 4 servings*

Nutrients per Serving: Calories: 410, Total Fat: 8g, Saturated Fat: 5g, Protein: 26g, Carbohydrate: 61g, Cholesterol: 25mg, Fiber: 2g, Sodium: 590mg

Mediterranean Pita Sandwiches

1 cup plain nonfat Greek yogurt
1 tablespoon chopped fresh cilantro
2 cloves garlic, minced
1 teaspoon lemon juice
1 can (about 15 ounces) chickpeas, rinsed and drained
1 can (14 ounces) artichoke hearts, rinsed, drained and
    coarsely chopped
1½ cups thinly sliced cucumber halves (halved lengthwise)
½ cup shredded carrots
½ cup chopped green onions
4 whole wheat pita bread rounds, cut in half

1. Combine yogurt, cilantro, garlic and lemon juice in small bowl; mix well.

2. Combine chickpeas, artichokes, cucumbers, carrots and green onions in medium bowl. Stir in yogurt mixture until well blended. Divide evenly among pita halves.   *Makes 4 servings*

Nutrients per Serving (2 filled pita halves): Calories: 420, Total Fat: 5g, Saturated Fat: 1g, Protein: 23g, Carbohydrate: 77g, Cholesterol: 0mg, Fiber: 8g, Sodium: 1210mg

Greek Chicken Burgers with Cucumber Yogurt Sauce

½ cup plus 2 tablespoons plain nonfat Greek yogurt
½ medium cucumber, peeled, seeded and finely chopped
  Juice of ½ lemon
3 cloves garlic, minced, divided
2 teaspoons finely chopped fresh mint *or* ½ teaspoon dried mint
⅛ teaspoon salt
⅛ teaspoon white pepper
1 pound ground chicken breast
3 ounces reduced-fat crumbled feta cheese
4 large kalamata olives, rinsed, patted dry and minced
½ to 1 teaspoon dried oregano
¼ teaspoon black pepper
1 egg
  Mint leaves or mixed baby lettuce (optional)

1. For sauce, combine yogurt, cucumber, lemon juice, 2 cloves minced garlic, mint, salt and white pepper in medium bowl; mix well. Refrigerate until ready to serve.

2. Combine chicken, feta, olives, oregano, black pepper and remaining garlic in large bowl; mix well.

3. Beat egg in small bowl. Add to chicken mixture; mix well. Shape into four patties.

4. Spray grill pan with nonstick cooking spray; heat over medium-high heat. Grill patties 5 to 7 minutes per side or until cooked through (165°F).

5. Top each burger with sauce. Garnish with mint and mixed greens.

Makes 4 servings

Nutrients per Serving (1 burger and ¼ of sauce): Calories: 260, Total Fat: 14g, Saturated Fat: 5g, Protein: 29g, Carbohydrate: 4g, Cholesterol: 150mg, Fiber: 1g, Sodium: 500mg

Diner Egg Salad Sandwiches

6 eggs
1½ tablespoons plain nonfat Greek yogurt
1½ tablespoons light mayonnaise
1½ tablespoons sweet pickle relish
½ cup finely chopped celery
⅛ to ¼ teaspoon salt
Black pepper (optional)
8 slices whole grain bread

1. Place eggs in medium saucepan; add cold water to cover. Bring to a boil over high heat. Reduce heat to low; simmer 10 minutes. Drain and peel eggs under cold water.

2. Cut eggs in half. Discard four egg yolk halves or reserve for another use. Place remaining egg yolks in medium bowl. Add yogurt, mayonnaise and pickle relish; mash with fork until well blended and creamy.

3. Chop egg whites; add to yolk mixture with celery and salt. Stir until well blended. Season with pepper, if desired.

4. Spread ½ cup egg salad on each of four bread slices; top with remaining bread slices.   *Makes 4 servings*

Nutrients per Serving (1 sandwich): Calories: 260, Total Fat: 10g, Saturated Fat: 3g, Protein: 17g, Carbohydrate: 26g, Cholesterol: 280mg, Fiber: 4g, Sodium: 470mg

Beef Stew Stroganoff

2 tablespoons olive or canola oil

1½ pounds lean boneless beef (bottom round), cut into 1-inch cubes

1 teaspoon caraway seeds

½ teaspoon salt

½ teaspoon black pepper

½ teaspoon dried thyme

2 cans (about 14 ounces each) reduced-sodium fat-free beef broth

1 cup sliced mushrooms

½ cup thinly sliced carrots

½ cup chopped red bell pepper

6 ounces unpeeled baby red potatoes, quartered (about 6 small)

¼ cup plain nonfat Greek yogurt

1. Heat oil in large saucepan over medium-high heat. Add beef; cook and stir until meat begins to brown. Add caraway seeds, salt, black pepper and thyme; cook and stir 1 minute.

2. Add broth, stirring to scrape up browned bits from bottom of saucepan. Bring to a boil over medium-high heat. Stir in mushrooms, carrots and bell pepper. Reduce heat to low; cover and simmer 1 hour.

3. Add potatoes; bring to a boil over high heat. Reduce heat to low; cover and simmer 20 minutes. Stir in yogurt; cook 2 minutes or until heated through.   *Makes 6 servings*

Nutrients per Serving (⅙ of total recipe): Calories: 230, Total Fat: 10g, Saturated Fat: 4g, Protein: 29g, Carbohydrate: 7g, Cholesterol: 70mg, Fiber: 1g, Sodium: 520mg

Lemon Broccoli Pasta

3 tablespoons sliced green onions

1 clove garlic, minced

2 cups reduced-sodium vegetable broth

1½ teaspoons grated lemon peel

⅛ teaspoon black pepper

2 cups fresh or frozen broccoli florets

3 ounces uncooked angel hair pasta

⅓ cup plain nonfat Greek yogurt

2 tablespoons grated reduced-fat Parmesan cheese

1. Generously spray large saucepan with cooking spray; heat over medium heat. Add green onions and garlic; cook and stir 3 minutes or until green onions are tender.

2. Stir broth, lemon peel and pepper into saucepan; bring to a boil over high heat. Stir in broccoli and pasta; return to a boil. Reduce heat to low; simmer, uncovered, 6 to 7 minutes or until pasta is tender, stirring frequently.

3. Remove from heat; stir in yogurt until well blended. Let stand 5 minutes. Sprinkle with cheese before serving. *Makes 6 servings*

Nutrients per Serving (1 cup): Calories: 120, Total Fat: 1g, Saturated Fat: 0g, Protein: 6g, Carbohydrate: 20g, Cholesterol: 0mg, Fiber: 2g, Sodium: 125mg

Curried Veggie Burgers

  2 eggs
  ⅓ cup plain nonfat Greek yogurt
  2 teaspoons vegetarian Worcestershire sauce
  2 teaspoons curry powder
  ½ teaspoon salt
  ¼ teaspoon ground red pepper
1⅓ cups cooked couscous or brown rice
  ½ cup finely chopped walnuts
  ½ cup grated carrots
  ½ cup minced green onions
  ⅓ cup plain dry bread crumbs
  4 sesame seed hamburger buns
    Honey mustard
    Thinly sliced cucumber or apple

1. Spray grid with nonstick cooking spray; prepare grill for direct cooking.

2. Combine eggs, yogurt, Worcestershire sauce, curry powder, salt and red pepper in large bowl; stir until blended. Add couscous, walnuts, carrots, green onions and bread crumbs; mix well. Shape into four 1-inch-thick patties.

3. Grill patties over medium-high heat 5 to 6 minutes per side or until heated through. Serve on buns with mustard and cucumber.

Makes 4 servings

Nutrients per Serving (1 sandwich): Calories: 470, Total Fat: 16g, Saturated Fat: 3g, Protein: 15g, Carbohydrate: 64g, Cholesterol: 95mg, Fiber: 4g, Sodium: 860mg

Note: Burgers can be broiled 4 inches from heat source for 5 to 6 minutes per side or until heated through.

Chicken Salad Pitas with Yogurt Sauce

1½ cups diced cooked chicken breast
½ cup red seedless grapes, halved if large
1 stalk celery, chopped
2½ tablespoons plain nonfat Greek yogurt
2 tablespoons fat-free mayonnaise
¼ teaspoon salt
⅛ teaspoon chili powder
⅛ teaspoon curry powder
⅛ teaspoon black pepper
2 whole wheat pitas, cut in half
4 pieces leaf lettuce
1 tablespoon sliced almonds

1. Combine chicken, grapes and celery in medium bowl. Combine yogurt, mayonnaise, salt, chili powder, curry powder and pepper in small bowl; mix well. Add to chicken mixture; toss gently to coat.

2. Split each pita half open and line with lettuce leaf. Spoon ½ cup chicken mixture into each pita half; sprinkle with sliced almonds.

Makes 4 servings

Nutrients per Serving (1 pita half with ½ cup filling): Calories: 178, Total Fat: 3g, Saturated Fat: 1g, Protein: 20g, Carbohydrate: 20g, Cholesterol: 41mg, Fiber: 3g, Sodium: 410mg

Greek Lamb with Tzatziki Sauce

2½ to 3 pounds boneless leg of lamb
8 cloves garlic, divided
¼ cup Dijon mustard
2 tablespoons minced fresh rosemary leaves
2 teaspoons salt
2 teaspoons black pepper
¼ cup plus 2 teaspoons olive oil, divided
1 small seedless cucumber
1 tablespoon chopped fresh mint
1 teaspoon lemon juice
2 cups plain nonfat Greek yogurt

1. Untie and unroll lamb to lie flat; trim fat.

2. For marinade, mince 4 garlic cloves; place in small bowl. Add mustard, rosemary, salt and pepper; whisk in ¼ cup olive oil. Spread mixture evenly over lamb, coating both sides. Place lamb in large resealable food storage bag. Seal bag; refrigerate at least 2 hours or overnight, turning several times.

3. Meanwhile, prepare Tzatziki Sauce. Mince remaining 4 garlic cloves and mash to a paste; place in medium bowl. Peel and grate cucumber; squeeze to remove excess moisture. Add cucumber, mint, remaining 2 teaspoons olive oil and lemon juice to bowl with garlic. Add yogurt; mix well. Refrigerate until ready to serve.

4. Prepare grill for direct cooking. Grill lamb over medium-high heat 35 to 40 minutes or to desired doneness. Cover loosely with foil; let rest 5 to 10 minutes. (Remove from grill at 140°F for medium. Temperature will rise 5°F while resting.)

5. Slice lamb and serve with Tzatziki Sauce. *Makes 8 servings*

Nutrients per Serving (⅛ of total recipe): Calories: 360, Total Fat: 22g, Saturated Fat: 8g, Protein: 32g, Carbohydrate: 6g, Cholesterol: 90mg, Fiber: 0g, Sodium: 850mg

SOUPS, SALADS & SIDES

Spicy Pumpkin Soup with Green Chile Swirl

1 can (4 ounces) diced green chiles
¼ cup plain nonfat Greek yogurt
¼ cup fresh cilantro leaves
1 can (15 ounces) solid-pack pumpkin
1 can (about 14 ounces) fat-free reduced-sodium chicken
    or vegetable broth
½ cup water
1 teaspoon ground cumin
½ teaspoon chili powder
¼ teaspoon garlic powder
⅛ teaspoon ground red pepper (optional)
    Additional plain nonfat Greek yogurt (optional)

1. Combine chiles, ¼ cup yogurt and cilantro in food processor or blender; process until smooth.*

2. Combine pumpkin, broth, water, cumin, chili powder, garlic powder and red pepper, if desired, in medium saucepan. Stir in ¼ cup green chile mixture; bring to a boil over high heat. Reduce heat to medium; simmer, uncovered, 5 minutes, stirring occasionally.

3. Ladle into four bowls. Top each serving with small dollops of remaining green chile mixture and additional yogurt, if desired. Run tip of spoon through dollops to swirl. *Makes 4 servings*

Or add chiles directly to soup. Finely chop cilantro and stir into yogurt. Top soup with dollops of yourt-cilantro mixture as directed.

Nutrients per Serving: Calories: 60, Total Fat: 1g, Saturated Fat: 0g, Protein: 3g, Carbohydrate: 11g, Cholesterol: 0mg, Fiber: 4g, Sodium: 350mg

Chicken & Pasta Caesar Salad

4 small boneless skinless chicken breasts

6 ounces uncooked potato gnocchi or other dried pasta

1 package (9 ounces) frozen artichoke hearts, thawed

1½ cups cherry tomatoes, quartered

¼ cup plus 2 tablespoons plain nonfat Greek yogurt

2 tablespoons light mayonnaise

2 tablespoons grated Romano cheese

1 tablespoon sherry or red wine vinegar

1 clove garlic, minced

½ teaspoon anchovy paste

½ teaspoon Dijon mustard

½ teaspoon white pepper

1 small head romaine lettuce, torn into bite-size pieces

1 cup toasted bread cubes

1. Grill or broil chicken breasts until no longer pink in center.

2. Cook pasta according to package directions, omitting salt. Drain and rinse under cold water. Combine pasta, artichokes and tomatoes in large bowl.

3. Combine yogurt, mayonnaise, cheese, sherry, garlic, anchovy paste, mustard and pepper in small bowl; whisk until smooth. Add to pasta mixture; toss gently to coat.

4. Arrange lettuce on serving plates; top with pasta salad, chicken and bread cubes. *Makes 4 main-dish servings*

Nutrients per Serving: Calories: 370, Total Fat: 9g, Saturated Fat: 2g, Protein: 36g, Carbohydrate: 37g, Cholesterol: 85mg, Fiber: 9g, Sodium: 610mg

South Asian Curried Potato Salad

  2 pounds unpeeled red new potatoes
1½ teaspoons salt, divided
  ¾ cup plain nonfat Greek yogurt
  ½ cup diced onion
  ½ cup diced celery
  ⅓ cup diced green bell pepper
  ¼ cup light mayonnaise
  2 teaspoons curry powder
  2 teaspoons lemon juice

1. Combine potatoes and 1 teaspoon salt in large saucepan; add cold water to cover. Bring to a boil; boil 20 minutes or just until potatoes are tender. Drain potatoes; let cool to room temperature.

2. Combine yogurt, onion, celery, bell pepper, mayonnaise, curry powder, lemon juice and remaining ½ teaspoon salt in large bowl; mix well.

3. Cut potatoes into 1-inch pieces. Add potatoes to yogurt mixture; stir gently to coat. *Makes 10 servings*

Nutrients per Serving: Calories: 100, Total Fat: 2g, Saturated Fat: 0g, Protein: 3g, Carbohydrate: 17g, Cholesterol: 0mg, Fiber: 2g, Sodium: 410mg

Chilled Cantaloupe Soup
(pictured)

½ medium to large cantaloupe, rind removed, seeded, cut into cubes
¼ cup plain nonfat Greek yogurt
¾ cup half-and-half
   Salt and white pepper
   Slivered cantaloupe (optional)

1. Place cantaloupe in food processor or blender; process until smooth. Add yogurt; process until blended.

2. Pour cantaloupe mixture into medium bowl; stir in half-and-half. Season with salt and pepper. Refrigerate until ready to serve. Garnish with slivered cantaloupe. *Makes 4 servings*

Nutrients per Serving: Calories: 90, Total Fat: 5g, Saturated Fat: 4g, Protein: 3g, Carbohydrate: 8g, Cholesterol: 15mg, Fiber: 1g, Sodium: 35mg

Tropical Turkey Salad

4 cups cubed cooked turkey breast
2 cups diced ripe mango (2 medium mangoes)
1 cup pecan pieces, toasted (optional)
½ cup plain nonfat Greek yogurt
¼ cup light mayonnaise
1 tablespoon lime juice
1 teaspoon poppy seeds
½ teaspoon salt
¼ teaspoon black pepper
6 cups greens, such as Bibb lettuce or spinach leaves

1. Combine turkey, mangoes and pecans, if desired, in large bowl. Combine yogurt, mayonnaise, lime juice, poppy seeds, salt and pepper in small bowl; mix well. Add to turkey mixture; toss gently to coat.

2. Serve immediately on greens or cover and refrigerate up to 4 hours. *Makes 6 servings*

Nutrients per Serving: Calories: 230, Total Fat: 7g, Saturated Fat: 2g, Protein: 31g, Carbohydrate: 11g, Cholesterol: 70mg, Fiber: 1g, Sodium: 330mg

Shrimp and Spinach Salad

4 cups baby spinach

12 ounces medium cooked shrimp (with tails), chilled

1 small red onion, thinly sliced

1 cup cooked whole wheat penne pasta or macaroni

½ cup plain nonfat Greek yogurt

1 tablespoon white wine vinegar

1 tablespoon olive oil

1 clove garlic, minced

¼ teaspoon smoked paprika

¼ teaspoon dried oregano

¼ teaspoon black pepper

⅛ teaspoon salt (optional)

¼ cup feta cheese crumbles (optional)

1. Combine spinach, shrimp, onion and pasta in large bowl.

2. Whisk yogurt, vinegar, oil, garlic, paprika, oregano, pepper and salt, if desired, in small bowl. Add to shrimp mixture; toss gently to coat. Sprinkle with feta cheese, if desired.   *Makes 6 servings*

Nutrients per Serving (1 cup): Calories: 150, Total Fat: 3g, Saturated Fat: 0g, Protein: 18g, Carbohydrate: 11g, Cholesterol: 110mg, Fiber: 1g, Sodium: 616mg

Tip: Deep red smoked paprika is made from sweet Spanish red peppers that are slowly smoked over oak wood. In addition to salad dressings, its smoky flavor is wonderful in roasted vegetables, meats, seafood, soups and dips. It can be found in the spice aisle of most supermarkets as well as spice and gourmet shops.

Greek Chickpea Salad

4 cups packed baby spinach leaves
1 cup canned chickpeas, rinsed and drained
1 large shallot, thinly sliced
4 pitted kalamata olives, sliced
2 tablespoons crumbled reduced-fat feta cheese
¼ cup plain nonfat Greek yogurt
2 teaspoons white wine vinegar
1 small clove garlic, minced
1 teaspoon olive oil
¼ teaspoon black pepper
⅛ teaspoon salt

1. Combine spinach, chickpeas, shallot, olives and feta cheese in large bowl.

2. Whisk yogurt, vinegar, garlic, oil, pepper and salt in small bowl until well blended. Add to salad just before serving; toss gently to coat.

Makes 4 servings

Nutrients per Serving (1 cup): Calories: 115, Total Fat: 3g, Saturated Fat: 1g, Protein: 6g, Carbohydrate: 17g, Cholesterol: 2mg, Fiber: 4g, Sodium: 409mg

Curried Brown Rice with Beans and Yogurt

1¼ cups reduced-sodium chicken or vegetable broth

¾ cup uncooked quick-cooking brown rice

1½ teaspoons curry powder

⅛ teaspoon red pepper flakes

2 teaspoons canola oil

1 small onion, chopped (¾ cup)

1 cup canned no-salt-added kidney beans, rinsed and drained

1 cup canned no-salt-added chickpeas, rinsed and drained

1 cup canned no-salt-added pinto beans, rinsed and drained

1 teaspoon garlic salt

½ cup chopped cilantro, divided

½ cup plain low-fat Greek yogurt

1. Combine broth, rice, curry powder and red pepper flakes in medium saucepan; bring to a boil over high heat. Reduce heat to low; cover and simmer 10 to 12 minutes or until liquid is absorbed.

2. Meanwhile, heat oil in large nonstick skillet over medium-high heat. Add onion; cook and stir 5 minutes or until tender. Stir in beans and garlic salt; heat through.

3. Stir ¼ cup cilantro into rice. Divide among four serving plates; top with warm bean mixture, yogurt and remaining ¼ cup cilantro.

Makes 4 servings

Nutrients per Serving: Calories: 287, Total Fat: 7g, Saturated Fat: 2g, Protein: 14g, Carbohydrate: 44g, Cholesterol: 11mg, Fiber: 10g, Sodium: 512mg

Pumpkin-Apple Bisque

1 tablespoon canola oil

1 cup diced onion

1 cup diced red bell pepper

1 cup diced peeled Granny Smith apple

½ (15-ounce) can navy beans, rinsed and drained

2 cups reduced-sodium vegetable broth, divided

1 can (15 ounces) solid-pack pumpkin

3 tablespoons sugar

1½ teaspoons curry powder

½ teaspoon ground cumin

½ teaspoon ground nutmeg

⅛ to ¼ teaspoon ground red pepper

1½ cups fat-free half-and-half

½ to ¾ teaspoon salt

½ cup low-fat Greek yogurt

1. Heat oil in large saucepan over medium-high heat. Add onion, bell pepper and apple; cook and stir 4 to 6 minutes or until onion is soft.

2. Transfer onion mixture to blender. Add beans and 1 cup broth; blend until smooth. Return mixture to saucepan. Stir in remaining 1 cup broth, pumpkin, sugar, curry powder, cumin, nutmeg and red pepper; bring to a boil over high heat. Reduce heat to low; cover and simmer 20 minutes.

3. Remove from heat; stir in half-and-half and salt. Ladle into six bowls; top with yogurt.   *Makes 6 servings*

Nutrients per Serving (about 1 cup): Calories: 190, Total Fat: 5g, Saturated Fat: 1g, Protein: 8g, Carbohydrate: 33g, Cholesterol: 5mg, Fiber: 7g, Sodium: 470mg

Waldorf Salad
(pictured)

2 unpeeled tart red apples, such as McIntosh, coarsely chopped
2 teaspoons fresh lemon juice
2 tablespoons plus 2 teaspoons thawed frozen apple juice concentrate
2 tablespoons light mayonnaise
2 tablespoons plain nonfat Greek yogurt
¼ teaspoon paprika
1 cup finely chopped celery
  Lettuce leaves
¼ cup coarsely chopped walnuts

1. Combine apples and lemon juice in large bowl; toss to coat.

2. Combine apple juice concentrate, mayonnaise, yogurt and paprika in small bowl; mix well. Add to apple mixture with celery; toss to coat. Cover and refrigerate 2 hours before serving.

3. Serve salad over lettuce leaves; sprinkle with walnuts.

Makes 4 servings

Nutrients per Serving: Calories: 140, Total Fat: 7g, Saturated Fat: 1g, Protein: 2g, Carbohydrate: 19g, Cholesterol: 5mg, Fiber: 3g, Sodium: 70mg

Creamy Garlic Dressing

½ cup plain nonfat Greek yogurt
½ cup light mayonnaise
  Juice of 1 lemon
3 cloves garlic, minced
1 tablespoon red wine vinegar
  Salt and black pepper

Combine all ingredients in medium bowl; mix well.

Makes about 1 cup

Nutrients per Serving (2 tablespoons): Calories: 60, Total Fat: 5g, Saturated Fat: 1g, Protein: 1g, Carbohydrate: 3g, Cholesterol: 5mg, Fiber: 0g, Sodium: 105mg

Chilled Cucumber Soup

1 large cucumber, peeled, seeded and coarsely chopped
¾ cup plain nonfat Greek yogurt
¼ cup packed fresh dill
½ teaspoon salt (optional)
⅛ teaspoon white pepper (optional)
1½ cups fat-free reduced-sodium chicken or vegetable broth
4 fresh dill sprigs

1. Place cucumber in food processor; process until finely chopped. Add yogurt, ¼ cup dill, salt and pepper, if desired; process until smooth.

2. Transfer mixture to large bowl; stir in broth. Cover and refrigerate at least 2 hours or up to 24 hours. Ladle into bowls; garnish with dill sprigs.

Makes 4 servings

Nutrients per Serving (¾ cup): Calories: 35, Total Fat: 0g, Saturated Fat: 0g, Protein: 5g, Carbohydrate: 3g, Cholesterol: 0mg, Fiber: 1g, Sodium: 190mg

Tangy Blue Cheese Potato Salad

1 pound red new potatoes
⅓ cup reduced-fat crumbled blue cheese
¼ cup plain nonfat Greek yogurt
¼ cup light mayonnaise
1 tablespoon cider vinegar
⅛ teaspoon garlic powder
½ cup chopped celery

1. Place potatoes in medium saucepan; add cold water to cover. Bring to a boil over medium-high heat; boil until tender. Drain potatoes; cut into 1-inch chunks when cool enough to handle.

2. Combine blue cheese, yogurt, mayonnaise, vinegar and garlic powder in large bowl; mix well. Add potatoes and celery; toss gently to coat.

Makes 6 servings

Nutrients per Serving (¾ cup): Calories: 110, Total Fat: 5g, Saturated Fat: 2g, Protein: 3g, Carbohydrate: 14g, Cholesterol: 10mg, Fiber: 1g, Sodium: 150mg

Carrot Raisin Salad with Citrus Dressing

¾ cup plain nonfat Greek yogurt

¼ cup fat-free (skim) milk

1 tablespoon honey

1 tablespoon lime juice

1 tablespoon orange juice concentrate

Grated peel of 1 medium orange

¼ teaspoon salt

8 medium carrots, peeled and coarsely shredded (about 2 cups)

¼ cup raisins

⅓ cup chopped cashews

1. Combine yogurt, milk, honey, lime juice, orange juice concentrate, orange peel and salt in small bowl; mix well.

2. Combine carrots and raisins in large bowl. Add dressing; toss to coat. Cover and refrigerate 30 minutes. Toss again just before serving. Sprinkle with cashews.   *Makes 8 servings*

Nutrients per Serving: Calories: 100, Total Fat: 3g, Saturated Fat: 1g, Protein: 4g, Carbohydrate: 16g, Cholesterol: 0mg, Fiber: 2g, Sodium: 150mg

Salmon Pasta Salad
(pictured)

1 cup cooked medium pasta shells
1 can (6 ounces) canned red salmon, drained
½ cup finely chopped celery
2 tablespoons finely chopped red bell pepper
2 tablespoons chopped fresh parsley
1 green onion, finely chopped
1½ tablespoons plain nonfat Greek yogurt
1½ tablespoons fat-free mayonnaise
1 tablespoon lemon juice
2 teaspoons capers
⅛ teaspoon paprika

Combine all ingredients in medium bowl; mix well. Cover and refrigerate until ready to serve. *Makes 2 servings*

Nutrients per Serving (1½ cups): Calories: 240, Total Fat: 6g, Saturated Fat: 1g, Protein: 26g, Carbohydrate: 21g, Cholesterol: 70mg, Fiber: 2g, Sodium: 460mg

Creamy Avocado Dressing

2 ripe avocados, peeled and pitted
  Juice of 2 limes
2 tablespoons plain nonfat Greek yogurt
2 tablespoons extra virgin olive oil
1 teaspoon salt
½ teaspoon ground red pepper
½ teaspoon cumin

Combine all ingredients in food processor; process until smooth. Cover and refrigerate until ready to serve. *Makes about 1 cup*

Nutrients per Serving (2 tablespoons): Calories: 110, Total Fat: 11g, Saturated Fat: 2g, Protein: 1g, Carbohydrate: 5g, Cholesterol: 0mg, Fiber: 3g, Sodium: 300mg

Serving Suggestion: Use this dressing to top your favorite Tex-Mex salads, or use it as a dip for tortilla chips instead of guacamole.

Sweet Potato & Fruit Salad

2 sweet potatoes (8 ounces)
1 Granny Smith apple, unpeeled, chopped
¼ cup chopped celery
1 container (6 ounces) plain nonfat Greek yogurt
2 tablespoons orange juice
½ to 1 teaspoon grated fresh ginger
½ teaspoon curry powder
⅛ teaspoon salt
½ cup cinnamon-coated nuts, divided
¼ cup drained mandarin oranges

1. Pierce sweet potatoes in several places with fork. Place on microwavable plate; cover loosely with plastic wrap. Microwave on HIGH 6 to 7 minutes, turning halfway through cooking time. Cool completely.

2. Peel sweet potatoes and cut into 1-inch pieces. Combine sweet potatoes, apple and celery in large bowl.

3. Combine yogurt, orange juice, ginger, curry powder and salt in medium bowl. Add to sweet potato mixture; toss to coat. Add half of nuts; stir gently. Top with remaining nuts and oranges. Refrigerate until ready to serve.

Makes 4 to 6 servings

Nutrients per Serving: Calories: 180, Total Fat: 7g, Saturated Fat: 1g, Protein: 8g, Carbohydrate: 25g, Cholesterol: 0mg, Fiber: 5g, Sodium: 135mg

Variations: Any type of flavored nut will work in this salad, including honey-roasted or praline-coated varieties. For a spicier salad, stir in 1 tablespoon chopped jalapeño pepper.

BEST BAKING

Raspberry Corn Muffins

1 cup all-purpose flour
¾ cup cornmeal
½ cup sugar
2 teaspoons baking powder
½ teaspoon baking soda
½ teaspoon salt
⅔ cup plain nonfat Greek yogurt
⅓ cup fat-free (skim) milk
1 egg
¼ cup (½ stick) butter, melted
1¼ cups fresh or frozen raspberries

1. Preheat oven to 400°F. Line 12 standard (2½-inch) muffin cups with paper baking cups.

2. Combine flour, cornmeal, sugar, baking powder, baking soda and salt in large bowl. Combine yogurt, milk, egg and butter in medium bowl until well blended. Add yogurt mixture to flour mixture; stir just until blended. (Do not overmix.) Gently stir in raspberries. Spoon batter evenly into prepared muffin cups.

3. Bake 16 to 18 minutes or until toothpick inserted into centers comes out clean. Cool in pan 5 minutes; remove to wire rack to cool completely.

Makes 12 muffins

Nutrients per Serving (1 muffin): Calories: 160, Total Fat: 5g, Saturated Fat: 3g, Protein: 4g, Carbohydrate: 25g, Cholesterol: 25mg, Fiber: 2g, Sodium: 390mg

Chocolate Yogurt Snack Cake

⅔ cup plus 2 tablespoons unsweetened Dutch process cocoa powder, divided

1¾ cups all-purpose flour

2 teaspoons baking powder

1 teaspoon salt

½ teaspoon baking soda

1½ cups plain nonfat Greek yogurt, divided

½ cup low-fat buttermilk

1 teaspoon vanilla

1¼ cups granulated sugar

½ cup (1 stick) butter, softened

2 eggs

1 cup semisweet chocolate chips

½ cup powdered sugar, sifted

1. Preheat oven to 350°F. Spray 13×9-inch baking pan with nonstick cooking spray. Dust with 2 tablespoons cocoa; tap out excess.

2. Combine remaining ⅔ cup cocoa, flour, baking powder, salt and baking soda in medium bowl. Whisk 1 cup yogurt, buttermilk and vanilla in small bowl until well blended.

3. Beat granulated sugar and butter in large bowl with electric mixer at medium speed about 2 minutes or until light and fluffy. Add eggs; beat 2 minutes. Gradually add flour mixture; beat at low speed just until combined. Add yogurt mixture; beat 1 minute, scraping down side of bowl once. Pour batter into prepared pan.

4. Bake 25 to 30 minutes or until toothpick inserted into center comes out clean. Cool completely in pan on wire rack.

5. For frosting, place chocolate chips and remaining ½ cup yogurt in medium microwavable bowl. Microwave on HIGH 30 seconds; stir. Continue microwaving at 10-second intervals until chocolate is melted and mixture is smooth. Whisk in powdered sugar until well blended. Spread over cooled cake. Cut into 24 pieces. *Makes 24 servings*

Nutrients per Serving (1 piece): Calories: 170, Total Fat: 7g, Saturated Fat: 4g, Protein: 4g, Carbohydrate: 27g, Cholesterol: 25mg, Fiber: 2g, Sodium: 220mg

Loaded Banana Bread

 6 tablespoons (¾ stick) butter, softened
⅓ cup granulated sugar
⅓ cup packed brown sugar
 2 eggs
 2 ripe bananas, mashed
½ cup plain low-fat Greek yogurt
½ teaspoon vanilla
1½ cups all-purpose flour
2½ teaspoons baking powder
¼ teaspoon salt
 1 can (8 ounces) crushed pineapple, drained
⅓ cup flaked coconut
¼ cup mini chocolate chips
⅓ cup chopped walnuts (optional)

1. Preheat oven to 350°F. Spray 9×5-inch loaf pan with nonstick cooking spray.

2. Beat butter, granulated sugar and brown sugar in large bowl with electric mixer at medium speed until light and fluffy. Beat in eggs, one at a time, beating well after each addition. Add bananas, yogurt and vanilla; beat just until combined.

3. Sift flour, baking powder and salt into small bowl. Gradually beat flour mixture into banana mixture just until combined. Fold in pineapple, coconut and chocolate chips. Spoon batter into prepared pan. Sprinkle with walnuts, if desired.

4. Bake 50 minutes or until toothpick inserted into center comes out almost clean. Cool in pan 1 hour; remove to wire rack to cool completely.

Makes 12 servings

Nutrients per Serving (1 slice): Calories: 230, Total Fat: 9g, Saturated Fat: 5g, Protein: 4g, Carbohydrate: 35g, Cholesterol: 45mg, Fiber: 2g, Sodium: 230mg

Mini Confetti Whoopie Pies

2 cups all-purpose flour
1 teaspoon baking powder
1 teaspoon baking soda
½ teaspoon salt
½ cup granulated sugar
½ cup packed brown sugar
½ cup vegetable oil
1 egg
2 teaspoons vanilla, divided
½ cup plus 2 tablespoons plain low-fat Greek yogurt, divided
½ cup reduced-fat (2%) milk
3 tablespoon rainbow sprinkles, divided
2 cups powdered sugar
1 cup (2 sticks) butter, softened

1. Preheat oven to 350°F. Line cookie sheets with parchment paper.

2. Combine flour, baking powder, baking soda and salt in medium bowl. Combine granulated sugar, brown sugar, oil, egg and 1 teaspoon vanilla in large bowl; stir with wooden spoon until well blended. Add ½ cup yogurt, milk and flour mixture; stir just until blended.

3. Spoon half teaspoonfuls of batter 2 inches apart on prepared cookie sheets. Sprinkle with 1 tablespoon sprinkles.

4. Bake 8 minutes or until lightly browned around edges. Remove to wire racks to cool completely.

5. For filling, beat powdered sugar, butter, remaining 2 tablespoons yogurt and 1 teaspoon vanilla in large bowl with electric mixer at medium speed until smooth and fluffy.

6. Spread filling on flat side of half of cookies; top with remaining cookies. Place remaining 2 tablespoons sprinkles in shallow bowl. Roll edges of cookies in sprinkles.   *Makes 40 mini whoopie pies*

Nutrients per Serving (1 whoopie pie): Calories: 120, Total Fat: 5g, Saturated Fat: 3g, Protein: 1g, Carbohydrate: 17g, Cholesterol: 15mg, Fiber: 0g, Sodium: 115mg

Berry-Peachy Cobbler

4 tablespoons plus 2 teaspoons sugar, divided

¾ cup plus 2 tablespoons all-purpose flour, divided

1¼ pounds peaches, peeled and sliced *or* 1 package (16 ounces) frozen unsweetened sliced peaches, thawed and drained

2 cups fresh raspberries *or* 1 package (12 ounces) frozen unsweetened raspberries

1 teaspoon grated lemon peel

½ teaspoon baking powder

½ teaspoon baking soda

⅛ teaspoon salt

2 tablespoons cold butter, cut into small pieces

¼ cup plus 1 tablespoon low-fat buttermilk

¼ cup plain nonfat Greek yogurt

1. Preheat oven to 425°F. Spray eight ramekins or 11×7-inch baking dish with nonstick cooking spray; place ramekins in jelly-roll pan.

2. Combine 2 tablespoons sugar and 2 tablespoons flour in large bowl. Add peaches, raspberries and lemon peel; toss to coat. Divide fruit evenly among prepared ramekins. Bake 15 minutes or until fruit is bubbly around edges.

3. Meanwhile, combine remaining ¾ cup flour, 2 tablespoons sugar, baking powder, baking soda and salt in medium bowl. Cut in butter with pastry blender or two knives until mixture resembles coarse crumbs. Stir in buttermilk and yogurt just until dry ingredients are moistened.

4. Remove ramekins from oven; top fruit with equal dollops of topping. Sprinkle topping with remaining 2 teaspoons sugar. Bake 18 to 20 minutes or until topping is lightly browned. Serve warm.   *Makes 8 servings*

Nutrients per Serving: Calories: 150, Total Fat: 3g, Saturated Fat: 2g, Protein: 3g, Carbohydrate: 29g, Cholesterol: 10mg, Fiber: 3g, Sodium: 180mg

Pumpkin Chocolate Chip Muffins

2½ cups all-purpose flour
 1 tablespoon baking powder
1½ teaspoons pumpkin pie spice*
 ½ teaspoon salt
 1 cup solid-pack pumpkin
 1 cup packed brown sugar
 ½ cup fat-free (skim) milk
 2 eggs
 6 tablespoons butter, melted
 ¼ cup plain nonfat Greek yogurt
 1 cup semisweet chocolate chips
 ½ cup chopped walnuts (optional)

*Or substitute ¾ teaspoon ground cinnamon, ½ teaspoon ground ginger and ¼ teaspoon each ground allspice and ground nutmeg.

1. Preheat oven to 400°F. Line 18 standard (2½-inch) muffin cups with paper baking cups or spray with nonstick cooking spray.

2. Combine flour, baking powder, pumpkin pie spice and salt in large bowl. Beat pumpkin, brown sugar, milk, eggs, butter and yogurt in medium bowl until well blended. Add pumpkin mixture, chocolate chips and walnuts, if desired, to flour mixture; stir just until moistened. Spoon evenly into prepared muffin cups, filling two-thirds full.

3. Bake 15 minutes or until toothpick inserted into centers comes out clean. Cool in pans 10 minutes; remove to wire racks to cool completely.

Makes 18 muffins

Nutrients per Serving (1 muffin): Calories: 160, Total Fat: 7g, Saturated Fat: 5g, Protein: 4g, Carbohydrate: 21g, Cholesterol: 30mg, Fiber: 1g, Sodium: 190mg

Naan (Indian Flatbread)

1 package (¼ ounce) active dry yeast
1 teaspoon sugar
¼ cup plus 2 tablespoons warm water, divided
3 cups all-purpose flour
1 teaspoon salt
1 teaspoon kalonji* seeds or poppy seeds (optional)
½ cup plain whole milk Greek yogurt
¼ cup (½ stick) melted butter, plus additional butter for brushing
   on naan

Kalonji seed is often called onion seed or black cumin seed. It is available in Indian markets and is traditional in some varieties of naan.

1. Stir yeast and sugar into 2 tablespoons water in small bowl. Let stand 10 minutes or until foamy. Place flour, salt and kalonji, if desired, in bowl of stand mixer. Attach dough hook; stir until blended.

2. Add yeast mixture, yogurt and ¼ cup butter; mix at low speed until combined. Add remaining ¼ cup water by tablespoonfuls, mixing at low speed until dough comes together and cleans side of bowl. (You may not need all the water.) Knead at low speed 5 to 7 minutes or until dough is smooth and elastic.

3. Shape dough into ball and place in greased bowl, turning to grease top. Let rise in warm place 1½ to 2 hours or until doubled.

4. Punch dough down; divide into 6 pieces. Roll into balls and place on plate sprayed with nonstick cooking spray. Cover and let rest 10 to 15 minutes.

5. Meanwhile, prepare grill for direct cooking or preheat oven to 500°F with baking stone on rack in lower third of oven. (Remove other racks.)

6. Place each ball of dough on lightly floured surface; roll and stretch into ⅛-inch-thick oval. Place 2 or 3 dough ovals on grill or baking stone. Grill, covered, or bake 2 minutes until puffed. Turn, brush with butter and grill or bake 1 to 2 minutes until browned in patches on both sides. Brush with butter; serve warm.   *Makes 12 servings*

Nutrients per Serving (½ naan): Calories: 165, Total Fat: 5g, Saturated Fat: 3g, Protein: 5g, Carbohydrate: 25g, Cholesterol: 13mg, Fiber: 1g, Sodium: 230mg

Blueberry Yogurt Cake

1 cup chopped walnuts
½ cup packed brown sugar
1 teaspoon ground cinnamon
1 cup applesauce
½ cup granulated sugar
¼ cup (½ stick) butter, softened
2 eggs
1 teaspoon vanilla
1½ cups cake flour
1 teaspoon baking powder
¼ teaspoon baking soda
½ cup plain nonfat Greek yogurt
1 cup fresh or frozen blueberries
1 teaspoon all-purpose flour

1. Preheat oven to 350°F. Line 8-inch square baking pan with foil; spray with nonstick cooking spray.

2. Combine walnuts, brown sugar and cinnamon in small bowl. Sprinkle one third of mixture over bottom of prepared pan.

3. Beat applesauce, granulated sugar and butter in large bowl with electric mixer at medium speed 2 minutes. Beat in eggs and vanilla until blended. Sift cake flour, baking powder and baking soda into medium bowl. Add to applesauce mixture with yogurt; beat until smooth.

4. Toss blueberries with all-purpose flour in small bowl; gently fold into batter. Pour half of batter over walnut mixture in prepared pan. Sprinkle with one third of walnut mixture; top with remaining batter and walnut mixture.

5. Bake 30 to 35 minutes or until toothpick inserted into center comes out clean. Cool completely in pan on wire rack.   *Makes 16 servings*

Nutrients per Serving (1 piece): Calories: 200, Total Fat: 9g, Saturated Fat: 3g, Protein: 4g, Carbohydrate: 28g, Cholesterol: 35mg, Fiber: 1g, Sodium: 170mg

Three-Fruit Crumble

1 large sweet apple (such as Jonagold or Gala), peeled and cut into
    1-inch pieces
1 large ripe pear, peeled and cut into 1-inch pieces
½ cup fresh cranberries
2 tablespoons apricot fruit spread
1 tablespoon sugar substitute*
½ teaspoon ground cinnamon, divided
⅛ teaspoon salt
⅛ teaspoon ground ginger
1 tablespoon water
1 teaspoon all-purpose flour
½ cup high-fiber cereal with small clusters
¼ cup old-fashioned oats
2 teaspoons packed brown sugar
1 tablespoon margarine, cut into small pieces
⅓ cup plain nonfat Greek yogurt
1½ teaspoons granulated sugar
⅛ teaspoon vanilla

This recipe was tested using sucralose-based sugar substitute.

1. Preheat oven to 350°F. Spray 8-inch square baking dish with nonstick cooking spray.

2. For filling, combine apple, pear, cranberries, fruit spread, sugar substitute, ¼ teaspoon cinnamon, salt and ginger in large bowl. Stir water into flour in small bowl. Add to fruit mixture; mix well. Spoon into prepared baking dish.

3. For topping, combine cereal, oats, brown sugar and remaining ¼ teaspoon cinnamon in medium bowl. Add margarine; mix with fingers to form coarse crumbs. Sprinkle over fruit.

4. Bake 40 to 45 minutes or until fruit is tender and bubbly and topping is golden brown.

5. Combine yogurt, granulated sugar and vanilla in small bowl until well blended. Spoon crumble into four bowls; top with dollop of yogurt mixture.

Makes 4 servings

Nutrients per Serving (⅔ cup): Calories: 169, Total Fat: 4g, Saturated Fat: 1g, Protein: 3g, Carbohydrate: 34g, Cholesterol: <1mg, Fiber: 4g, Sodium: 158mg

Chile Corn Bread

1 teaspoon canola or olive oil
¼ cup chopped red bell pepper
¼ cup chopped green bell pepper
2 small jalapeño peppers,* minced
2 cloves garlic, minced
¾ cup corn (fresh or thawed frozen)
1½ cups yellow cornmeal
½ cup all-purpose flour
2 tablespoons sugar
2 teaspoons baking powder
½ teaspoon baking soda
½ teaspoon ground cumin
½ teaspoon salt
1 cup plain nonfat Greek yogurt
½ cup fat-free (skim) milk
2 eggs
¼ cup (½ stick) butter, melted

*Jalapeño peppers can sting and irritate the skin, so wear rubber gloves when handling peppers and do not touch your eyes.

1. Preheat oven to 375°F. Spray 8-inch square baking pan with nonstick cooking spray.

2. Heat oil in small skillet over medium heat. Add bell peppers, jalapeño peppers and garlic; cook and stir over medium heat 3 to 4 minutes or until peppers are tender. Stir in corn; cook 1 to 2 minutes. Remove from heat.

3. Combine cornmeal, flour, sugar, baking powder, baking soda, cumin and salt in large bowl. Add yogurt, milk, eggs and butter; stir until blended. Stir in corn mixture. Pour batter into prepared pan.

4. Bake 25 to 30 minutes or until toothpick inserted into center comes out clean. Cool in pan on wire rack.   *Makes 12 servings*

Nutrients per Serving (1 piece): Calories: 160, Total Fat: 5g, Saturated Fat: 3g, Protein: 5g, Carbohydrate: 23g, Cholesterol: 40mg, Fiber: 2g, Sodium: 520mg

DREAMY CREAMY DESSERTS

Little Lemon Basil Pops

1¼ cups plain nonfat Greek yogurt
¼ cup fat-free (skim) milk
Grated peel and juice of 1 lemon
2 tablespoons sugar
2 tablespoons chopped fresh basil
Ice cube trays
Pop sticks

1. Combine yogurt, milk, lemon peel, lemon juice, sugar and basil in blender or food processor; blend until smooth.

2. Pour mixture into ice cube trays. Freeze 2 hours.

3. Insert sticks. Freeze 4 to 6 hours or until firm.

4. To remove pops from trays, place bottoms of ice cube trays under warm running water until loosened. Press firmly on bottoms to release. (Do not twist or pull sticks.) *Makes 16 pops*

Nutrients per Serving (1 pop): Calories: 20, Total Fat: 0g, Saturated Fat: 0g, Protein: 2g, Carbohydrate: 3g, Cholesterol: 0mg, Fiber: 0g, Sodium: 10mg

Double Berry Pops

2 cups plain nonfat Greek yogurt, divided
1 cup blueberries
3 tablespoons sugar, divided
   Paper or plastic cups or pop molds
1 cup sliced strawberries
   Pop sticks

1. Combine 1 cup yogurt, blueberries and 1½ tablespoons sugar in blender or food processor; blend until smooth.

2. Pour mixture into cups. Freeze 2 hours.

3. Combine strawberries, remaining 1 cup yogurt and 1½ tablespoons sugar in blender or food processor; blend until smooth.

4. Pour mixture into cups over blueberry layer. Cover top of each cup with small piece of foil. Freeze 2 hours.

5. Insert sticks through center of foil. Freeze 4 hours or until firm.

6. To serve, remove foil and peel away paper cups or gently twist frozen pops out of plastic cups.   *Makes 6 pops*

Nutrients per Serving (1 pop): Calories: 90, Total Fat: 0g, Saturated Fat: 0g, Protein: 7g, Carbohydrate: 15g, Cholesterol: 0mg, Fiber: 1g, Sodium: 30mg

Cinnamon-Honey Pops

1¼ cups plain nonfat Greek yogurt
½ cup honey
¼ cup fat-free (skim) milk
1 tablespoon sugar
½ teaspoon ground cinnamon
½ teaspoon vanilla
   Pop molds or paper or plastic cups
   Pop sticks

1. Combine yogurt, honey, milk, sugar, cinnamon and vanilla in blender or food processor; blend until smooth.

2. Pour mixture into molds. Cover top of each mold with small piece of foil. Freeze 2 hours.*

3. Insert sticks through center of foil. Freeze 4 hours or until firm.

4. To remove pops from molds, remove foil and place bottoms of pops under warm running water until loosened. Press firmly on bottoms to release. (Do not twist or pull sticks.)   *Makes 6 pops*

If using pop molds with lids, skip step 3 and freeze until firm.

Nutrients per Serving (1 pop): Calories: 120, Total Fat: 0g, Saturated Fat: 0g, Protein: 5g, Carbohydrate: 28g, Cholesterol: 0mg, Fiber: 0g, Sodium: 25mg

Summer Berry-Custard Pie

9 whole graham crackers
¼ cup egg whites
2 tablespoons butter, melted and cooled
1 cup low-fat (1%) milk
½ cup sugar substitute*
1 egg
3 tablespoons cornstarch
Pinch salt
1½ cups plain low-fat Greek yogurt
2 teaspoons vanilla
1½ cups fresh blueberries or raspberries (or a combination)

*This recipe was tested using sucralose-based sugar substitute.

1. Preheat oven to 350°F. Spray 9-inch glass pie plate with nonstick cooking spray.

2. For crust, place graham crackers in food processor; process until finely ground. Transfer to medium bowl; stir in egg whites and butter. Press mixture onto bottom and up side of prepared pie plate. Bake 10 minutes. Cool completely.

3. For filling, combine milk, sugar substitute, egg, cornstarch and salt in medium saucepan. Cook over medium heat 5 to 8 minutes or until mixture boils and thickens, whisking constantly. Remove from heat; stir in yogurt and vanilla.

4. Spoon filling into crust; press plastic wrap onto surface of filling. Refrigerate 4 hours or until firm. Top with fresh berries just before serving.

Makes 8 servings

Nutrients per Serving: Calories: 176, Total Fat: 6g, Saturated Fat: 3g, Protein: 8g, Carbohydrate: 24g, Cholesterol: 42mg, Fiber: 1g, Sodium: 154mg

Patriotic Pops

¾ cup plain nonfat Greek yogurt
2 tablespoons lemon juice, divided
1 tablespoon fat-free (skim) milk
1 cup sliced strawberries
½ cup blueberries
  Pop molds
  Pop sticks

1. Combine yogurt, 1 tablespoon lemon juice and milk in blender or food processor; blend until smooth.

2. Combine remaining 1 tablespoon lemon juice and strawberries in blender or food processor; blend until smooth.

3. Alternately layer blueberries, yogurt mixture and strawberry mixture in molds.* Cover top of each mold with small piece of foil. Insert sticks through center of foil. Freeze 4 hours or until firm.

4. To remove pops from molds, remove foil and place bottoms of pops under warm running water until loosened. Press firmly on bottoms to release. (Do not twist or pull sticks.) *Makes 4 servings*

Plastic pop molds must be used for this recipe. The fruit will not stay in place if using paper or plastic cups.

Nutrients per Serving (1 pop): Calories: 50, Total Fat: 0g, Saturated Fat: 0g, Protein: 4g, Carbohydrate: 8g, Cholesterol: 0mg, Fiber: 1g, Sodium: 20mg

Blackberry Layered Pops

1¼ cups plain nonfat Greek yogurt, divided
¼ cup fat-free (skim) milk
2 tablespoons sugar, divided
2 tablespoons lime juice, divided
1 cup chopped blackberries, divided
   Pop molds or paper or plastic cups
   Pop sticks

1. Combine ¾ cup yogurt, milk, 1 tablespoon sugar and 1 tablespoon lime juice in blender or food processor; blend until smooth. Gently stir in ¼ cup blackberries.

2. Pour mixture into molds. Freeze 1 hour.

3. Combine ½ cup blackberries and 1½ teaspoons lime juice in blender or food processor; blend until smooth.

4. Pour mixture into molds over yogurt layer. Freeze 1 hour.

5. Combine remaining ½ cup yogurt, ¼ cup blackberries, 1 tablespoon sugar and 1½ teaspoons lime juice in blender or food processor; blend until smooth.

6. Pour mixture into molds over blackberry layer. Cover top of each mold with small piece of foil. Insert sticks through center of foil. Freeze 4 hours or until firm.

7. To remove pops from molds, remove foil and place bottoms of pops under warm running water until loosened. Press firmly on bottoms to release. (Do not twist or pull sticks.)   *Makes 4 pops*

Nutrients per Serving (1 pop): Calories: 80, Total Fat: 0g, Saturated Fat: 0g, Protein: 7g, Carbohydrate: 14g, Cholesterol: 0mg, Fiber: 2g, Sodium: 35mg

Cherry Parfait Crunch

12 ounces dark or light sweet cherries
½ cup unsweetened apple juice
¼ teaspoon ground cinnamon
    Dash ground nutmeg
1 teaspoon cornstarch
1 tablespoon water
⅓ cup natural wheat and barley cereal
2 tablespoons chopped toasted almonds
2 cups vanilla nonfat Greek yogurt

1. Remove stems and pits from cherries; cut into halves (about 2¼ cups).

2. Combine cherries, apple juice, cinnamon and nutmeg in small saucepan; cook and stir over medium heat 5 minutes or until cherries begin to soften.

3. Stir cornstarch into water in small bowl until smooth; stir into saucepan. Cook over high heat until mixture boils and thickens slightly, stirring constantly. Let cool 10 minutes; cover and refrigerate until chilled.

4. Combine cereal and almonds in small bowl. Layer half of cherry mixture, half of yogurt and half of cereal mixture in four parfait glasses; repeat layers.   *Makes 4 servings*

Nutrients per Serving (1 parfait): Calories: 210, Total Fat: 2g, Saturated Fat: 0g, Protein: 13g, Carbohydrate: 37g, Cholesterol: 0mg, Fiber: 2g, Sodium: 100mg

Apricot Pops

1 can (about 8 ounces) apricot halves in heavy syrup
1 cup apricot nectar
½ cup plain nonfat Greek yogurt
   Pop molds or paper or plastic cups
   Pop sticks

1. Drain apricots; discard syrup. Rinse apricots under cool water; drain and chop.

2. Combine apricot nectar, yogurt and ¼ cup chopped apricots in blender or food processor; blend until smooth. Stir in remaining chopped apricots.

3. Pour mixture into molds. Cover top of each mold with small piece of foil. Freeze 1 hour.*

4. Insert sticks through center of foil. Freeze 4 hours or until firm.

5. To remove pops from molds, remove foil and place bottoms of pops under warm running water until loosened. Press firmly on bottoms to release. (Do not twist or pull sticks.)   *Makes 4 pops*

If using pop molds with lids, skip step 4 and freeze until firm.

Nutrients per Serving (1 pop): Calories: 90, Total Fat: 0g, Saturated Fat: 0g, Protein: 3g, Carbohydrate: 22g, Cholesterol: 0mg, Fiber: 1g, Sodium: 15mg

Raspberry Layered Pops

1¼ cups plain nonfat Greek yogurt, divided
¼ cup fat-free (skim) milk
2 tablespoons sugar, divided
2 tablespoons lemon juice, divided
1 cup chopped raspberries, divided
    Paper or plastic cups or pop molds
    Pop sticks

1. Combine ¾ cup yogurt, milk, 1 tablespoon sugar and 1 tablespoon lemon juice in blender or food processor; blend until smooth. Gently stir in ¼ cup raspberries.

2. Pour mixture into cups. Freeze 1 hour.

3. Combine ½ cup raspberries and 1½ teaspoons lemon juice in blender or food processor; blend until smooth.

4. Pour mixture into cups over yogurt layer. Freeze 1 hour.

5. Combine remaining ½ cup yogurt, ¼ cup raspberries, 1 tablespoon sugar and 1½ teaspoons lemon juice in blender or food processor; blend until smooth

6. Pour mixture into cups over raspberry layer. Cover top of each cup with small piece of foil. Insert sticks through center of foil. Freeze 4 hours or until firm.

7. To serve, remove foil and peel away paper cups or gently twist frozen pops out of plastic cups. *Makes 4 pops*

Nutrients per Serving (1 pop): Calories: 80, Total Fat: 0g, Saturated Fat: 0g, Protein: 7g, Carbohydrate: 14g, Cholesterol: 0mg, Fiber: 2g, Sodium: 35mg

No-Bake Ginger-Lime Yogurt Pie

3 cups plain nonfat Greek yogurt
4 ounces reduced-fat cream cheese, softened
1 envelope unflavored gelatin
¼ cup water
½ cup sugar substitute*
2 to 4 tablespoons minced crystallized ginger
1 teaspoon grated lime peel
1 (6-ounce) reduced-fat graham cracker crust
4 cups fresh blueberries, raspberries or sliced strawberries
Crystallized ginger strips (optional)

*This recipe was tested using sucralose-based sugar substitute.

1. Beat yogurt and cream cheese in medium bowl with electric mixer at medium speed until light and fluffy.

2. Sprinkle gelatin over water in medium saucepan; let stand 2 minutes to soften. Stir in sugar substitute. Cook over medium heat about 1 minute or until mixture thickens slightly and gelatin dissolves, stirring constantly. (Do not boil.)

3. Add gelatin mixture, minced ginger and lime peel to yogurt mixture; stir until well blended. Spoon filling into crust; press plastic wrap onto surface of filling. Refrigerate at least 4 hours or until firm. Serve with berries; garnish with ginger strips. *Makes 8 to 10 servings*

Nutrients per Serving: Calories: 216, Total Fat: 6g, Saturated Fat: 2g, Protein: 12g, Carbohydrate: 30g, Cholesterol: 30mg, Fiber: 4g, Sodium: 193mg

Note: Crystallized ginger is available in large supermarkets and Asian markets. It is moist and chewy with a spicy-sweet flavor. Store it in an airtight container in a cool, dark place for up to 3 months.

Chocolate Chip Frozen Yogurt

1 cup vanilla nonfat Greek yogurt
½ cup fat-free half-and-half
2 tablespoons sugar
¼ teaspoon vanilla
¼ cup mini chocolate chips

1. Combine yogurt, half-and-half, sugar and vanilla in medium bowl; mix well.

2. Freeze yogurt mixture in ice cream maker according to manufacturer's directions until soft. Add chocolate chips; freeze until firm.

Makes 4 servings

Nutrients per Serving (½ cup): Calories: 130, Total Fat: 4g, Saturated Fat: 2g, Protein: 6g, Carbohydrate: 20g, Cholesterol: 0mg, Fiber: 1g, Sodium: 55mg

Raspberry Cream Parfaits

1 cup plain low-fat Greek yogurt
2 teaspoons honey
¼ teaspoon vanilla
1 cup raspberry sorbet
2 cups fresh raspberries
1 (1-ounce) biscotti *or* 2 gingersnaps, crumbled

1. Whisk yogurt, honey and vanilla in small bowl until smooth.

2. Spoon 2 tablespoons yogurt mixture into each of four parfait glasses. Top with ¼ cup sorbet, ½ cup raspberries, 2 tablespoons yogurt mixture and cookie crumbs.

Makes 4 servings

Nutrients per Serving (1 parfait): Calories: 171, Total Fat: 3g, Saturated Fat: 1g, Protein: 7g, Carbohydrate: 33g, Cholesterol: 15mg, Fiber: 4g, Sodium: 55mg

Metric Conversion Chart

VOLUME MEASUREMENTS (dry)

1/8 teaspoon = 0.5 mL
1/4 teaspoon = 1 mL
1/2 teaspoon = 2 mL
3/4 teaspoon = 4 mL
1 teaspoon = 5 mL
1 tablespoon = 15 mL
2 tablespoons = 30 mL
1/4 cup = 60 mL
1/3 cup = 75 mL
1/2 cup = 125 mL
2/3 cup = 150 mL
3/4 cup = 175 mL
1 cup = 250 mL
2 cups = 1 pint = 500 mL
3 cups = 750 mL
4 cups = 1 quart = 1 L

VOLUME MEASUREMENTS (fluid)

1 fluid ounce (2 tablespoons) = 30 mL
4 fluid ounces (1/2 cup) = 125 mL
8 fluid ounces (1 cup) = 250 mL
12 fluid ounces (1 1/2 cups) = 375 mL
16 fluid ounces (2 cups) = 500 mL

WEIGHTS (mass)

1/2 ounce = 15 g
1 ounce = 30 g
3 ounces = 90 g
4 ounces = 120 g
8 ounces = 225 g
10 ounces = 285 g
12 ounces = 360 g
16 ounces = 1 pound = 450 g

DIMENSIONS

1/16 inch = 2 mm
1/8 inch = 3 mm
1/4 inch = 6 mm
1/2 inch = 1.5 cm
3/4 inch = 2 cm
1 inch = 2.5 cm

OVEN TEMPERATURES

250°F = 120°C
275°F = 140°C
300°F = 150°C
325°F = 160°C
350°F = 180°C
375°F = 190°C
400°F = 200°C
425°F = 220°C
450°F = 230°C

BAKING PAN SIZES

Utensil	Size in Inches/Quarts	Metric Volume	Size in Centimeters
Baking or Cake Pan (square or rectangular)	8×8×2	2 L	20×20×5
	9×9×2	2.5 L	23×23×5
	12×8×2	3 L	30×20×5
	13×9×2	3.5 L	33×23×5
Loaf Pan	8×4×3	1.5 L	20×10×7
	9×5×3	2 L	23×13×7
Round Layer Cake Pan	8×1½	1.2 L	20×4
	9×1½	1.5 L	23×4
Pie Plate	8×1¼	750 mL	20×3
	9×1¼	1 L	23×3
Baking Dish or Casserole	1 quart	1 L	—
	1½ quart	1.5 L	—
	2 quart	2 L	—